THE

WAR OF ANTICHRIST WITH THE CHURCH

AND

CHRISTIAN CIVILIZATION.

A REVIEW OF

THE RISE AND PROGRESS OF ATHEISM; ITS EXTENSION THROUGH VOLTAIRE; ITS USE OF
FREEMASONRY AND KINDRED SECRET SOCIETIES FOR ANTICHRISTIAN WAR;
THE UNION AND "ILLUMINISM" OF MASONRY BY WEISHAUPT; ITS PROGRESS UNDER THE
LEADERS OF THE FIRST FRENCH REVOLUTION, AND UNDER NUBIUS, PALMERSTON, AND MAZZINI;
THE CONTROL OF ITS HIDDEN "INNER CIRCLE" OVER ALL REVOLUTIONARY ORGANIZATIONS;
ITS INFLUENCE OVER BRITISH FREEMASONRY; ITS ATTEMPTS UPON IRELAND;
OATHS, SIGNS, AND PASSWORDS OF THE THREE DEGREES, ETC., ETC.
THE SPOLIATION OF THE PROPAGANDA.

LECTURES

DELIVERED IN EDINBURGH IN OCTOBER, 1884,

BY

MONSIGNOR GEORGE F. DILLON, D.D.,

MISSIONARY APOSTOLIC, SYDNEY.

*"Instruct the people as to the artifices used by societies of this kind in seducing men
and enticing them into their ranks, and as to the depravity of their opinions and the
wickedness of their acts."*—Encyclical Humanum Genus of Leo XIII.

DUBLIN:
M. H. GILL & SON, UPPER SACKVILLE-STREET.
LONDON AND NEW YORK: BURNS AND OATES.
1885.

FACSIMILE OF TITLE PAGE OF ORIGINAL EDITION
PUBLISHED BY
MESSRS. M. H. GILL & SON, DUBLIN,
IN 1885

GRAND ORIENT
FREEMASONRY
UNMASKED

As the Secret Power
Behind Communism

BY

MONSIGNOR GEORGE F. DILLON D.D.

SABAH

AKITA INC / Exterminatrix Imprints

MMXXI

DEDICATION

This work is dedicated to the memory of His Holiness Pope Leo XIII whose command to the faithful to "tear away the mask from Freemasonry" inspired the title of the new edition in 1950.

This current edition includes the dedication, publisher's forward, and conclusion of the 1950 edition of Britons Publishing Company.

CONTENTS

"Lying is their rule, Satan is their God, and shameful deeds their sacrifice." Pius VIII, Traditae Humilitati Nostrae, 1829.

Gregory XVI compares the secret societies to a sink in which "are congregated and intermingled all the sacrileges, infamy and blasphemy which are contained in the most abominable heresies." Gregory XVI, Mirari Vos, 1832.

"Those baneful secret sects which have come forth from the darkness for the ruin and devastation of Church and State," Pius IX, Quo Pluribus, 1846, to whom he later applied the words of Our Lord: *"You are from your father the devil, and it is the works of your father that you wish to do."* Pius IX, Singulari Quadam, 1864.

"You see then before you the two systems ... On the one side is the Church of 'men of goodwill,' one, holy, visible and universal; on the other, the ecclesia malignantium, as the Scriptures call it, the Church of men of evil will; one in enmity against the Church of God, though manifold as the multiplicity of evil; unholy in thought, word, deed, intention and will; invisible because secret, stealthy, subterraneous, working out of sight, and in darkness undermining the private purities of homes, the public order of States, the thrones of princes." Cardinal Manning: Rome and the Revolution, 1867.

"Filled with the spirit of Satan, who knows how to transform himself into an angel of light. Freemasonry puts forward as its pretended aim the good of humanity. Paying a lip service to the authority of law, and even to the obligations of religion, it aims (as its own statutes declare), at the destruction of civil authority and of the Christian priesthood, both of which it regards as the foes of human liberty." Leo XIII: Parvenu à la Vingtcinquième année, 1902.

PUBLISHER'S FOREWORD

The original title of this book, which was compiled from a series of lectures delivered in Edinburgh in October, 1884 by Mgr. Dillon, was *The War of Antichrist with the Church and Christian Civilization.*

The author wrote it "in order to do his part in carrying out the instruction given by the Sovereign Pontiff in the Encyclical Humanum Genus when he called upon the pastors of souls, to whom it was addressed, to 'instruct the people as to the artifices used by societies of this kind in seducing men and enticing them into their ranks, and as to the depravity of their opinions and the wickedness of their acts.'" Mgr. Dillon's work has already been honoured by the Holy Father himself with so marked and so unusual an approbation that there is no need for us to accord it any further praise than merely to take note of the fact. The book was presented to His Holiness, accompanied by an Italian version of its table of contents, and of long extracts from its principal sections, and Leo XIII was pleased to order that the Italian version should be completed, and the book printed and published at Rome at his own expense." (*The Month*, Sept. 1885).

Despite the fact that the lectures were delivered by a Catholic prelate to an audience composed mainly of members of his own faith, we feel that the subject of international political skullduggery is one which cannot fail to interest Catholic and non-Catholic alike, the more so indeed since events in the course of the decades following the original publication of this book have confirmed the lecturer's thesis.

The last four editions have appeared under the title of *Grand Orient Freemasonry Unmasked.*

I

GOOD VERSUS EVIL

SPEAKING of the operative classes, Leo XIII says, in his celebrated Encyclical Humanum Genus: "Those who sustain themselves by the labour of their own hands, besides being by their very condition most worthy above all others of charity and consolation, are also especially exposed to the allurements of men whose ways lie in fraud and deceit. Therefore, they ought to be helped with the greatest possible kindness, and invited to join societies that are good, lest they be drawn away to others that are evil."

In this, as in all matters of importance, "to be forewarned is to be forearmed," and it is specially necessary to be forewarned when we have to contend with an adversary who uses secrecy, fraud and deceit. We shall see then, that all the organizations of Atheism appear at first as does their author, Satan, clothed in the raiment of angels of light, with their malignity, their Infidelity, and their ultimate designs always most carefully hidden. They come amongst all the faithful but more especially amongst young men, to seduce and to ruin them, never showing but when forced to do so, the cloven foot, and employing a million means to seem to be what they are not. It is, therefore, first of all, necessary to unmask them; and this is precisely what the Supreme Pontiff asks the pastors of the Universal Fold to do as the best means of destroying their influence, "But," he says in the Encyclical already quoted, "as it befits our pastoral office that we ourselves should point out some suitable way of proceeding, we wish it to be your rule, first of all, to tear away the mask from Freemasonry, and to let it be seen as it really is, and by instructions and pastoral letters to instruct the people as to the artifices used by societies of this kind in seducing men and enticing them into their ranks, and as to the depravity of their opinions and the wickedness of their acts."

In this extract the Holy Father makes special mention of Freemasonry; but, remember, not of Freemasonry only. He speaks of "other secret societies." These other secret societies are identical with Freemasonry, no matter by what name they may be called; and they are frequently the most depraved forms of Freemasonry. And though what is known in Great Britain as Freemasonry may not be so malignant as its kind is on the Continent—though it may have little or no hold at all upon the mass of Catholics in English-speaking countries, still we shall see that like every secret society in existence it is a danger for the nation and for individuals, and has hidden within it the same Atheism and hostility to Christianity which the worst Continental Freemasonry possesses. These it develops to the initiated in the higher degrees, and makes manifest to all the world in time. The truth is that every secret society is framed and adapted to make men the enemies of God and of his Church, and to subvert faith; and there is not one, no matter on what pretext it may be founded, which does not fall under the management of a supreme directory governing all the secret societies on earth. The one aim of this directory is to uproot Christianity, and the Christian social order as well as the Church from the world—in fact, to eradicate the name of Christ and the very Christian idea from the minds and the hearts of men. This it is determined to do by every means, but especially by fraud and force; that is by first using wiles and deceit until the Atheistic conspiracy grows strong enough for measures as violent and remorseless in all countries as it exercised in one country during the first French Revolution. I believe this secret Atheistic organisation to be nothing less than the evil which we have been long warned against by Our Blessed Lord

Himself, as the supreme conflict between the Church and Satan's followers. It is the commencement of the contest which must take place between Christ and Antichrist; and nothing therefore can be more necessary than that the elect of God should be warned of its nature and its aims. First we shall glance at the rise and the nature of Atheism itself and its rapid advance amongst those sections of Christians most liable from position and surroundings to be led astray by it; and then at the use it has made of Freemasonry for its propagandism, and for its contemplated destruction of Christianity. We shall see its depravity perfected by what is called Illuminism. And we shall see that however checked it may have been by the reaction consequent upon the excesses of its first Revolution, it has not only outlived that reaction, but has grown wiser for doing an evil more extended and more complete. We shall see how its chiefs have succeeded in mastering and directing every kind of secret association whether springing from itself or coming into existence by the force of its example only; and have used, and are using them all to its advantage. We shall see the sleepless vigilance which this organized Atheism exercises; and thus come to know that our best, our only resource, is to fly its emissaries, and draw nearer in affection and in effect to the teachings of the Church and her Supreme

Visible Head on earth who can never deceive us, and whom the hosts of Satan never can deceive. We shall see that the voice of the Vicar of Christ has been raised against secret associations from the beginning to this hour, and that the directions which we receive from that infallible voice can alone save us from the wiles and deceits of a conspiracy so formidable, so active, so malignant, and so dangerous.

II

THE RISE OF ATHEISM IN EUROPE

IN order, then, to comprehend thoroughly the nature of the conspiracy, it will be necessary to go back to the opening of the last century and contemplate the rise and advance of the Atheism and Anti-Christianity which it now spreads rapidly through the earth. As that century opened it disclosed a world suffering from a multitude of evils. The so-called Reformation, which arose and continued to progress during the two preceding centuries had well nigh run its course. The principle of private judgment introduced in apparent zeal for the pure worship and doctrine of Christ, had ended in leaving no part of the teaching of Christ unchallenged. It had rendered His Divinity disbelieved in, and His very existence doubted, by many who yet called themselves His followers. Socinus and his nephew had succeeded in binding the various groups of Polish and German Protestants in a league where nothing was required but undying hatred and opposition to the Catholic Church. Bayle threw doubt upon everything, and Spinosa destroyed the little respect left for the Deity in the system of Socinus, by introducing Pantheism to the world. In effect, both the Deists and the Pantheists of that period were Atheists. Whether they held that everything was God, or that God was not such a God as Christians hold Him to be, they did away with belief in the true God, and raised up an impossible being of their own imagination in His stead. In life, in conduct, and in adoration of God, they were practical Atheists, and soon manifested that hatred for the truth which the Atheist is sure to possess. Their theories made headway early in the century throughout Central Europe and England. Boling-broke, Shaftesbury, and the elite amongst the statesmen and literary aristocracy of the reign of Queen Anne were Infidels. Tindal, Collins, Wolston, Toland, and Chubbs were as advanced as Tom Payne was, later on, in the way of Atheism. But however much England and Germany had advanced their Protestantism to what was called Free-thinking, both were soon destined to be eclipsed in that sad progress by Catholic and monarchical France. France owes this evil pre-eminence to one individual, who, though largely assisted in his road to ruin by Bayle, and subsequently by association with English Infidels, had yet enough of innate wickedness in himself to outstrip them all. That individual was Voltaire.

III

VOLTAIRE

THE career of this abandoned, unhappy, but most extraordinary man is the subject of this chapter. It was in his day and by his means that Atheism became perfected, generalized, and organized for the destruction of Christianity, Christian civilization, and all religion. He was the first, and remains still, the greatest of its Apostles. There is not one of its dark principles which he did not teach and advocate; and from his writings, and by their means, the intellectual and every other form of war against the Catholic Church and the cause of Christ are carried on to this day and will be to the end. His real name was Francis Mary Arouet, but, for some reason which has never been clearly explained, he chose to call himself Voltaire. He was the son of good parents, and by position and education should have been an excellent Catholic. He was trained by the very Jesuits whom he afterwards so hated and persecuted. He was destined for the profession of the law, and made good progress in literary studies. But the corruption of the age in which he lived soon seized upon him, overmastered him, and bore him along in a current which in his case did not end in vice only, but in vice which sought its own justification in Infidelity. From the beginning, the fool said in his heart "there is no God," and in the days of Voltaire the number of these fools was indeed infinite. Never before was vice so rampant in countries calling themselves Christian. If the Gospel was preached at all in that age it was certainly to the poor; for the rich, as a rule—to which there were, thank God, many exceptions—seemed so sunk in vice as not to believe in a particle of it. The Courts of Europe were, in general, corrupt to the core; and the Court of the Most Christian King was perhaps the most abandoned, in a wide sense, of them all. The Court of Catherine of Russia a scene of unblushing lewdness. The Court of Frederick of Prussia was so corrupt, that it cannot be described without doing violence to decency, and even to humanity. The Regent Orleans and Louis XV had carried licence to such an extent as to render the Court of Versailles a veritable pandemonium. The vices of royalty infected the nobles and all others who were so unfortunate as to be permitted to frequent Courts. Vice, in fact, was the fashion, and numbers of all classes, not excepting the poorest, wallowed in it. As a consequence, the libertines of the period hated the Church, which alone, amidst the universal depravity, raised her voice for purity. They took up warmly, therefore, the movements which, within or without her pale, were likely to do her damage. With a sure instinct they sided in France with Gallicanism and Jansenism; and they welcomed the new Infidelity which came over from England and Germany, with unconcealed gladness. Voltaire appeared in French society at this most opportune moment for the advancement of their views. Witty, sarcastic, gay, vivacious, he soon made his way amongst the voluptuaries who then filled Paris. His conduct and habit of ridiculing religion and royalty brought him, however, into disfavour with the Government, and at the age of twenty-seven we find him in the Bastille. Liberated from this prison in 1727, but only on condition of exile, he crossed over to England, where he finally adopted those Infidel and anti-Christian principles which made him, for the half century through which he afterwards lived, what Crétineau-Joly[1] very justly calls "the most perfect incarnation of Satan that the world ever saw." The Society of Freemasons was just then

---

[1] *L'Église Romaine en face de la Révolution*, par J. Crétineau-Joly, ouvrage composé sur des documents inédits et orné des portraits de Leurs Saintetés Les Papes Pie VII. et Pie IX. dessinés per Stall. Paris, 1861.

perfected in London, and Voltaire at the instance of his Infidel associates joined one of its lodges; and he left England, where he had been during the years 1726-27 and '28, an adept in both Infidelity and Freemasonry. He returned to the Continent with bitterness rankling in his breast against Monarchical Government which had imprisoned and exiled him, against the Bastille where he was immured, and, above all, against the Catholic Church and her Divine Founder. Christ and His Church condemned his excesses and to the overthrow of both he devoted himself with an ardour and a malignity more characteristic, certainly, of a demon than of a man.

A master of French prose hardly ever equalled and never perhaps excelled, and a graceful and correct versifier, his writings against morality and religion grew into immense favour with the corrupt reading-public of his day. He was a perfect adept in the use of ridicule, and he employed it with remorseless and blasphemous force against everything pure and sacred. He had as little respect for the honour or welfare of his country as he had for the sanctity of religion. His ruffian pen attacked the fair fame of the Maid of Orleans with as little scruple as it cast shame upon the consecrated servants of Christ. For Christ he had but one feeling—eternal, contemptuous hatred. His watchword, the concluding lines of all his letters to his infidel confederates, was for fifty years *écrasons nous l'infame*, "let us crush the wretch," meaning Christ and his cause. This he boasted was his *delenda est Carthago*. And he believed he could succeed. "I am tired," said he, "of hearing it said that twelve men sufficed to establish Christianity, and I desire to show that it requires but one man to pull it down." A lieutenant of police once said to him that, notwithstanding all he wrote, he should never be able to destroy Christianity. "That is exactly what we shall see," he replied. Voltaire was never weary of using his horrible watch-word.

Upon the news of the suppression of the Jesuits reaching him, he exclaimed: "See, one head of the hydra has fallen. I lift my eyes to heaven and cry 'crush the wretch.'" We have from himself his reason for using these blasphemous words. He says, "I finish all my letters by saying '*Écrasons l'infame, écrasez l'infame.*' 'Let us crush the wretch, crush the wretch,' as Cato used one time to say, *Delenda est Carthago*, Carthage must be destroyed." Even at a time when the miscreant protested the greatest respect for religion to the Court of Rome, he wrote to Damilaville: "We embrace the philosophers, and we beseech them to inspire for the wretch all the horror which they can. Let us fall upon the wretch ably. That which most concerns me is the propagation of the faith of truth, and the making of the wretch vile, *Delenda est Carthago.*"

Certainly his determination was strong to do so; and he left no stone unturned for that end. He was a man of amazing industry; and though his vanity caused him to quarrel with many of his confreres, he had in his lifetime a large school of disciples, which became still more numerous after his death.

He sketched out for them the whole mode of procedure against the Church. His policy as revealed by the correspondence of Frederick II, and others[2]

---

[2] To show how early the confederates of Voltaire had determined upon the gradual impoverishment of the Church and the suppression of the Religious orders, the following letters from Frederick II, will be of use. In the first dated 13th August, 1775, the Monarch writes to the then very aged "Patriarch of Ferney," who had demanded the secularization of the Rhine ecclesiastical electorates and other episcopal benefices in Germany, as follows:—

"All you say concerning our German bishops is but too true; they grow fat upon the tithes of Sion. But you know, also, that in the Holy Roman Empire the ancient usage, the Bull of Gold, and other antique follies, cause abuses established to be respected. If we wish to diminish fanaticism we must not touch the bishops. But, if we manage to diminish the monks, especially the mendicant orders, the people will grow cold and less superstitious, they will permit the powers that be, to dispose of the bishops in the manner best suited to the good of each State. This is the only course to follow. To undermine silently and without noise the edifice of infatuation is to oblige it to fall of itself. The Pope, seeing the situation in which he finds himself, is obliged to give briefs and bulls as his dear sons demand of him. The power founded upon the ideal credit of the faith loses in proportion as the latter diminishes. If there were now found at the head of nations some ministers above vulgar prejudices, the Holy Father would become bankrupt. Without doubt posterity will enjoy the advantage of being able to think freely."

with him, was not to commence an immediate per-secution, but first to suppress the Jesuits and all Religious orders, and to secularize their goods; then to deprive the Pope of temporal authority, and the Church of property and state recognition. Primary and higher-class education of a lay and Infidel character was to be established, the principle of divorce affirmed, and respect for ecclesiastics lessened and destroyed. Lastly, when the whole body of the Church should be sufficiently weakened and Infidelity strong enough, the final blow was to be dealt by the sword of open, relentless persecution. A reign of terror was to spread over the whole earth, and to continue while a Christian should be found obstinate enough to adhere to Christianity. This, of course, was to be followed by a Universal Brotherhood without marriage, family, property, God, or law, in which all men would reach that level of social degradation aimed at by the disciples of Saint Simon, and carried into practice whenever possible, as attempted by the French Commune.

In the carrying out of his infernal designs against religion and society, Voltaire had as little scruple in using lying and hypocrisy as Satan himself is accredited with. In his attacks upon religion he falsified history and fact. He made a principle of lying, and taught the same vice to his followers. Writing to his disciple Theriot, he says (*Oeuvres*, vol. 52, p. 326): "Lying is a vice when it does evil. It is a great virtue when it does good. Be therefore more virtuous than ever. It is necessary to lie like a devil, not timidly and for a time, but boldly and always."

He was also, as the school he left behind has been ever since, a hypocrite. Infidel to the heart's core, he could, whenever it suited his purpose, both practice, and even feign a zeal for religion. On the expectation of a pension from the King, he wrote to M. Axgental, a disciple of his, who reproached him with his hypocrisy and contradictions in conduct. "If I had a hundred thousand men I know well what I would do; but as I have not got them I will go to communion at Easter and you may call me a hypocrite as long as you like." And Voltaire, on getting his pension, went to communion the year following.[3] It is needless to say that he was in life, as well as in his writings, immoral as it was possible for a man to be.

---

[3] In 1768 Voltaire wrote as follows to the Marquis de Villevielle:—"No, my dear Marquis, no, the modern Socrates will not drink the hemlock. The Socrates of Athens was, between you and me, a pitiless caviller, who made himself a thousand enemies and who braved his judges very foolishly.

"Our modern philosophers are more adroit. They have not the foolish and dangerous vanity to put their names to their works. Theirs are the invisible hands which pierce fanaticism from one end of Europe to the other with the arrows of truth. Damilaville recently died. He was the author of 'Christianism unveiled,' and many other writings. No one ever knew him."

He lived without shame and even ostentatiously in open adultery. He laughed at every moral restraint. He preached libertinage and practised it. He was the guest and the inmate of the Court of Frederick of Prussia, where crime reached proportions impossible to speak of. And lastly, coward, liar, hypocrite, and panderer to the basest passions of humanity, he was finally, like Satan, a murderer if he had the power to be so. Writing to Damilaville, he says, "The Christian religion is an infamous religion, an abominable hydra which must be destroyed by a hundred invisible hands. It is necessary that the philosophers should course through the streets to destroy it as missionaries course over earth and sea to propagate it. They ought to dare all things, risk all things, even to be burned, in order to destroy it. Let us crush the wretch! Crush the wretch!" His doctrine thus expressed found fatal effect in the French Revolution, and it will obtain effect whenever his disciples are strong enough in men and means to act. I have no doubt his teachings have led to all the revolutions of this century, and will lead to the final attack of Atheism on the Church. Nor was his hatred confined to Catholicism only. Christians of every denomination were marked out for destruction by him; and our separated Christian brethren, who feel glad at seeing his followers triumph over the Church, might well ponder on these words of his: "Christians," he says, "of every form of profession, are beings exceedingly injurious, fanatics, thieves, dupes, imposters, who lie together with their gospels, enemies of the human race." And of the system itself he writes: "The Christian religion is evidently false, the Christian religion is a sect which every good man ought to hold in horror. It cannot be approved of even by those to whom it gives power and honour." In fact, since his day, it has been a cardinal point of policy with his followers to take advantage of the unfortunate differences between the various sects of Christians in the world and the Church, in order to ruin both; for the destruction of every form of Christianity, as well as Catholicism, was the aim of Voltaire, and remains as certainly the aim of his disciples. They place, of course, the Church and the Vicar of Christ in the first line of attack, well knowing that if the great Catholic unity could be destroyed, the work of eradicating every kind of separated Christianity would be easy. In dealing, therefore, with such a foe as modern Atheism, so powerfully organized, as we shall see it to be, Protestants as well as Catholics should guard against its wiles and deceits. They should, at least, regarding questions such as the religious education of rising generations, the attempted secularisation of the Sabbath and state-established

Christian Institutions, and the recognition of religion by the State, all of which the Atheism of the world now attempts to destroy, present an unbroken front of determined union. Nothing less, certainly, can save even the Protestantism, the national, Christian character of Great Britain and her colonies from impending ruin.

Although Voltaire was as confirmed and malignant a hater of Christ and of Christianity as ever lived, still he showed from time to time that his own professed principles of Infidelity were never really believed in by himself. In health and strength he cried out his blasphemous "crush the wretch!" but when the moment came for his soul to appear before the judgment-seat of "the wretch," his faith was shown and his vaunted courage failed him.

The miscreant always acted against his better knowledge. His life gives us many examples of this fact. I will relate one for you. When he broke a blood vessel on one occasion, he begged his assistants to hurry for the priest. He confessed, signed with his hand a profession of faith, asked pardon of God and the Church for his offences, and ordered that his retraction should be printed in the public newspapers; but, recovering, he commenced his war upon God anew, and died refusing all spiritual aid, and crying out in the fury of despair and agony, "I am abandoned by God and man." Dr. Fruchen, who witnessed the awful spectacle of his death, said to his friends, "Would that all who had been seduced by the writings of Voltaire had been witness of his death, it would be impossible to hold out, in the face of such an awful spectacle."[4] But that spectacle was forgotten, and consequently, before ten years passed, the world saw the effects of his works.

Speaking of the French Revolution, Condorcet, in his "Life of Voltaire," says of him, "He did not see all that which he accomplished, but he did all that which we see. Enlightened observations prove to those who know how to reflect that the first author of that Great Revolution was without doubt Voltaire."

It never was the intention of this man to let his teachings die, or beat the air, so to speak, with mere words. He determined that his fatal gospel should be perpetuated, and should bring forth as speedy as possible its fruits of death. Even in his lifetime, we have evidence that he constantly conspired with his associates for this end, and that with them he concocted in secret both the means by which his doctrines should reach all classes in Europe, and the methods by which civil order and Christianity might

---

[4] See *Le Secret de la Franc-Maçonnerie*, by Mgr. A. J. Fava, Bishop of Grenoble, Lille, 1883, p. 38.

be best destroyed. St. Beuve writes of him and of his, in the *Journal des Débats*, 8 November, 1852:—"All the correspondence of Voltaire and D'Alembert is ugly. It smells of the sect, of the conspiracy of the Brotherhood, of the secret society. From whatever point it is viewed it does no honour to men who make a principle of lying, and who consider contempt of their kind the first condition necessary to enlighten them. "'Enlighten and despise the human race.' A sure watchword this, and it is theirs. 'March on always sneering, my brethren, in the way of truth.' That is their perpetual refrain." But not only did he and his thus conspire in a manner which might seem to arise naturally from identical sentiments and aims, but what was of infinitely greater consequence, the demon, just as their sad gospel was ripe for propagation, called into existence the most efficacious means possible for its extension amongst men, and for the wished-for destruction of the Church, of Christian civilization, and of every form of existing Christianity. This was the spread amongst those already demoralized by Voltaireanism, of Freemasonry and its cognate systems of secret Atheistic organisation.

IV

FREEMASONRY

FREEMASONRY, we must remember always, appeared generally and spread generally, too, in the interests of all that Voltaire aimed at, when it best suited his purpose. The first lodge established in France under the English obedience was in 1727. Its founder and first master was the celebrated Jacobite, Lord Derwentwater. It had almost immediate acceptance from the degenerate nobility of France, who, partly because of the influence of English and Scotch Jacobite nobles, and partly because of its novelty, hard swearing, and mystery, joined the strange institution. Its lodges were soon in every considerable city of the realm. The philosophers and various schools of Atheists, however, were the first to enter into and to extend it. For them it had special attractions and special uses, which they were not slow to appreciate and to employ. Now, though it very little concerns us to know much of the origin of this society, which became then and since so notorious throughout the world, still, as that origin throws some light on its subsequent history, it will not be lost time to glance at what is known, or supposed to be known, about it. Mgr. Ségur,[1] Bishop of Grenoble, who devoted much time to a study of Freemasonry, is persuaded that it was first elaborated by Faustus Socinus, the nephew of the too celebrated Laelius Socinus, the heresiarch and founder of the sect of Unitarians or, as they are generally called after him, Socinians. Both were of the ancient family of the Sozini of Sienna. Faustus, like many of his relatives, imbibed the errors of his uncle, and in order to escape the vigilance of the Inquisition, to which both Italy and Spain owed much of the tranquility they enjoyed in these troublesome times, he fled to France. While in that country at Lyons, and when only twenty years of age, he heard of the death of his uncle at Zurich, and went at once to that city to obtain the papers and effects of the deceased. From the papers he found that Laelius had assisted at a conference of Heretics at Vicenza in 1547, in which the destruction of Christianity was resolved upon, and where resolutions were adopted for the renewal of Arianism—a system of false doctrine calculated to sap the very foundations of existing Faith by attacking the Trinity and the Incarnation. Feller, an

[1] Opus cit. p. 8.

authority of considerable weight, in his reference to this conference, says: "In the assembly of Vicenza they agreed upon the means of destroying the religion of Jesus Christ, by forming a society which by its progressive successes brought on, towards the end of the eighteenth century, an almost general apostasy. When the Republic of Venice became informed of this conspiracy, it seized upon Julian Trevisano and Francis de Rugo, and strangled them, Ochinus and the others saved themselves. The society thus dispersed became only the more dangerous, and it is that which is known to-day under the name of Freemasons." For this information Feller refers us to a work entitled *Le Voile Levé*, by the Abbé Le Franc, a victim of the reign of terror in 1792. The latter tells us that the conspirators whom the severity of the Venetian Republic had scattered, and who were Ochinus, Laelius Socinus, Peruta, Gentilis, Jacques Chiari, Francis Lenoir, Darius Socinus, Alicas, and the Abbé Leonard, carried their poison with them, and caused it to bear fruits of death in all parts of Europe. The success of Faustus Socinus in spreading his uncle's theories was enormous. His aim was not only to destroy the Church, but to raise up another temple into which any enemy of orthodoxy might freely enter. In this temple every heterodox belief might be held. It was called Christian but was without Christian faith, or hope, or love. It was simply an astutely planned system for propagating the ideas of its founders; for a fundamental part of the policy of Socinus, and one in which he well instructed his disciples, was to associate either to Unitarianism or to the confederation formed at Vicenza, the rich, the learned, the powerful, and the influential of the world. He feigned an equal esteem for Trinitarians and anti-Trinitarians, for Lutherans and Calvinists. He praised the undertakings of all against the Church of Rome, and working upon their intense hatred for Catholicism, caused them to forget their many "isms" in order to unite them for the destruction of the common enemy. When that should be effected, it would be time to consider a system agreeable to all. Until then, unity of action inspired by hatred of the Church should reign amongst them.

He therefore wished that all his adherents should, whether Lutheran or Calvinist, treat one another as brothers; and hence his disciples have been called at various times "United Brethren," "Polish Brothers," "Moravian Brothers," "Brother Masons," and finally "Freemasons." Mgr. Ségur informs us, on the authorities before quoted, as well as upon that of Bergier, and the learned author of a work entitled, *Les Francs-Maçons Écrasés*—the Abbé Lerudan—printed at Amsterdam, as early as the year 1747, that the real secret of Freemasonry consisted, even then, in disbelief in the Divinity of Christ, and a determination to replace that doctrine, which is the very foundation of Christianity, by Naturalism or Rationalism. Socinus having established his Sect in Poland, sent emissaries to preach his doctrines stealthily in Germany, Holland, and England. In Germany, Protestants and Catholics united to unmask them. In Holland they blended with the Anabaptists, and in England they found partisans amongst the Independents and various other sects into which the people were divided.

The Abbé Lefranc believes (*Le Voile Levé*, Lyons, 1821), that Oliver Cromwell was a Socinian, and that he introduced Freemasonry into England. Certainly, Cromwell's sympathies were not for the Church favoured by the monarch he supplanted, and were much with the Independents. If he was a Socinian, we can easily understand how the secret society of Vicenza could have attractions for one of his anti-Catholic and ambitious sentiments. He gave its members in England, as Mgr. Ségur tells us, the title of Freemasons, and invented the allegory of the Temple of Solomon, now so much used by Masonry of every kind, and which meant the original state of man supposed to be a commonwealth of equality with a vague Deism as its religion. This temple, destroyed by Christ for the Christian order, was to be restored by Freemasonry after Christ and the Christian order should be obliterated by conspiracy and revolution. The state of Nature was the "Hiram" whose murder Masonry was to avenge; and which, having previously removed Christ, was to resuscitate Hiram, by re-building the temple of Nature as it had been before.

Mgr. Ségur, moreover, connects modern Freemasonry with the Jews and Templars, as well as with Socinus. There are reasons which lead me to think that he is right in doing so. The Jews for many centuries previous to the Reformation had formed secret societies for their own protection and for the destruction of the Christianity which persecuted them, and which they so much hated. The rebuilding of the Temple of Solomon was the dream of their lives. It is unquestionable that they wished to make common cause with other bodies of persecuted religionists. They had special reason to welcome with joy such heretics as were cast off by Catholicism. It is, therefore, not at all improbable that they admitted into their secret conclaves some at least of the discontented Templars, burning for revenge upon those who dispossessed and suppressed the Order. That fact would account for the curious combination of Jewish and conventual allusions to be found in modern Masonry.[2] Then, as to its British History, we have seen that numbers of the secret brotherhood of Socinus made their way to England and Scotland, where they found rich friends, and, perhaps, confederates. I have, therefore, no doubt but that the Abbé Lefranc is correct when he says that Cromwell was connected with them. At least, before he succeeded in his designs, he had need of some such secret society, and would, no doubt, be glad to use it for his purposes. But it is not so clear that Cromwell was the first, as Lefranc thinks, to blend that brotherhood with the real Freemasons. The ancient guild of working masons had existed in Great Britain and in Europe for many centuries

---

[2] Gougenot des Mousseaux, in his work *Le Juif, le Judaïsme et la Judaïsation des Peuples Chrétiens* (Paris 1869), has brought together a great number of indications on the relations of the high chiefs of Masonry with Judaism. He thus concludes:—"Masonry, that immense association, the rare initiates of which, that is to say, the real chiefs of which, whom we must be careful not to confound with the nominal chiefs, live in a strict and intimate alliance with the militant members of Judaism, princes and imitators of the high Cabal. For that elite of the order—these real chiefs whom so few of the initiated know, or whom they only know for the most part under a *nom de guerre*, are employed in the profitable and secret dependence of the cabalistic Israelites. And this phenomenon is accomplished thanks to the habits of rigorous discretion to which they subject themselves by oaths and terrible menaces; thanks also to the majority of Jewish members which the mysterious constitution of Masonry seats in its sovereign counsel."

M. Crétineau-Joly gives a very interesting account of the correspondence between Nubius and an opulent German Jew who supplied him with money for the purposes of his dark intrigues against the Papacy. The Jewish connection with modern Freema-

previous to his time. They were like every other guild of craftsmen—a body formed for mutual protection and trade offices. But they differed from other tradespeople in this, that from their duties they were more cosmopolitan, and knew more of the ceremonies of religion at a period when the arts of reading and writing were not very generally understood. They travelled over every portion of England and Scotland, and frequently crossed the Channel, to work at the innumerable religious houses, castles, fortifications, great abbeys, churches and cathedrals which arose over the face of Christendom in such number and splendour in the middle and succeeding ages. To keep away interlopers, to sustain a

sonry is an established fact everywhere manifested in its history. The Jewish formulas employed by Masonry, the Jewish traditions which ran through its ceremonial, point to a Jewish origin, or to the work of Jewish contrivers. It is easy to conceive how such a society could be thought necessary to protect them from Christianity in power. It is easy also to understand how the one darling object of their lives is the rebuilding of the Temple. Who knows but behind the Atheism and desire of gain which impels them to urge on Christians to persecute the Church and to destroy it, there lies a hidden hope to reconstruct their Temple, and at the darkest depths of secret society plotting there lurks a deeper society still which looks to a return to the land of Juda and to the re-building of the Temple of Jerusalem. One of the works which Antichrist will do, it is said, is to re-unite the Jews, and to proclaim himself as their long looked-for Messias. As it is now generally believed that he is to come from Masonry and to be of it, this is not improbable, for in it he will find the Jews the most inveterate haters of Christianity, the deepest plotters, and the fittest to establish his reign.

uniform rate of wages, to be known amongst strangers, and, above all, amongst foreigners of their craft, signs were necessary; and these signs could be of value only in proportion to the secrecy with which they were kept within the craft itself. They had signs for those whom they accepted as novices, for the companion mason or journeyman, and for the masters of the craft. In ages when a trade was transmitted from father to son, and formed a kind of family inheritance, we can very well imagine that its secrets were guarded with much jealousy, and that its adepts were enjoined not to communicate them to anyone, not even to their wives, lest they become known to outsiders. The masons were, if we except the clockmakers and jewellers, the most skilled artisans of Europe. By the cunning of their hands they knew how to make the rough stone speak out the grand conceptions of the architects of the middle ages; and often, the delicate foliage and flowers and statuary of the fanes they built, remind us of the most perfect eras of Greek and Roman sculpture. So closely connected with religion and religious architecture as were these "Brothers Masons," "Friars," "Fra," or "Free Masons," they shared to a large extent in the favour of the Popes. They obtained many and valuable charters. But they degenerated. The era of the so-called Reformation was a sad epoch for them. It was an era of Church demolition rather than of Church building. Wherever the blight of Protestantism fell, the beauty and stateliness of Church architecture became dwarfed, stunted, and degraded, whenever it was not utterly destroyed. The need of Brothers Masons had passed, and succeeding Masons began to admit men to their guilds who won a living otherwise than by the craft. In Germany their confraternity had become a cover for the reformers, and Socinus, seeing it as a means for advancing his Sect—a method for winning adepts and progressing stealthily without attracting the notice of Catholic government—would desire no doubt to use it for his purposes. We have to this day the statute the genuine Freemasons of Strasbourg framed in 1462, and the same revised as late as 1563, but in them there is absolutely nothing of heresy or hostility to the Church. But there is a curious document called the Charter of Cologne dated 1535, which, if it be genuine, proves to us that there existed at that early period a body of Freemasons having principles identical with those professed by the Masons of our own day. It is to be found in the archives of the Mother Lodge of Amsterdam which also preserves the act of its own constitution under the date of 1519. It reveals the existence of lodges of kindred intent in London, Edinburgh, Vienna, Amsterdam,

Paris, Lyons, Frankfurt, Hamburg, Antwerp, Rotterdam, Madrid, Venice, Goriz, Koenigsberg, Brussels, Dantzig, Magdeburg, Bremen and Cologne; and it bears the signatures of well-known enemies of the Church at that period, namely—Hermanus or Herman de Weir, the immoral and heretical Archbishop-Elector of Cologne, placed for his misdeeds under the ban of the Empire; De Coligny, leader of the Huguenots of France; Jacob d'Anville, Prior of the Augustinians of Cologne, who incurred the same reproaches as Archbishop Herman; Melancthon, the Reformer; Nicholas Van Noot, Carlton, Bruce, Upson, Banning, Vireaux, Schroeder, Hoffman, Nobel, De la Torre, Doria, Uttenbow, Falck, Huissen, Wormer. These names reveal both the country and the celebrity of all the men who signed the document. It was, possibly, a society like theirs, which the Venetian Government broke up and scattered in 1547, for we find distinct mention of a lodge existing at Venice in 1535. However this may be. Freemason lodges existed in Scotland from the time of the Reformation. One of them is referred to in the Charter of Cologne, and doubtless had many affiliations. In Scotland, as in other Catholic countries, the Templars were suppressed; and there, if nowhere else, that Order had the guilds of working masons under its special protection. It is therefore possible, as some say, that the knights coalesced with these Masons, and protected their own machinations with the aid of the secrets of the craft. But while this and all else stated regarding the connection of the Templars with Masonry may be true, there is no real evidence that it is so. Much is said about the building of the Temple of Solomon; and that the Hiram killed, and whose death the craft is to avenge, means James Molay, the Grand Master, executed in the barbarous manner of his age for supposed complicity in the crimes with which the Templars were everywhere charged. There is tall talk about such things in modern Masonry, and a great deal of the absurd and puerile ritual in which the sect indulges when conferring the higher grades, is supposed to have reference to them. But the Freemasonry with which we have to deal, however connected in its origin with the Templars, with Socinus, with the conspirators of Cologne, or those of Vicenza, or with Cromwell, received its modern characteristics from Elias Ashmole, the Antiquary, and the provider, if not the founder, of the Oxford Museum. Ashmole was an alchemist and an astrologer, and imbued consequently with a love for the jargon and mysticism of that strange body so busied about the philosopher's stone and other Utopias. The existing lodges of the Freemasons had an inexpressible charm for Ashmole, and in 1646 he, together with Colonel Main-waring, became members of the craft. He perfected it, added various mystic symbols to those already in use and gave partly a scriptural, partly an Egyptian form to its jargon and ceremonies. The Rosecroix, Rosicrucian degree, a society formed after the idea of Bacon's New Atlantis, appeared; and the various grades of companion, master, secret master, perfect master, elect, and Irish master, were either remodelled or newly formed, as we know them now. Charles I was decapitated in 1649, and Ashmole being a Royalist to the core, soon turned English Masonry from the purposes of Cromwell and his party, and made the craft, which was always strong in Scotland, a means to upset the Government of the Protector and to bring back the Stuarts. Now "Hiram." became the murdered Charles, who was to be avenged instead of James Molay, and the reconstruction of the Temple meant the restoration of the exiled House of Stuart. On the accession of Charles II the craft was, of course, not treated with disfavour; and when the misfortunes of James II drove him from the throne, the partisans of the House of Stuart had renewed recourse to it as a means of secret organization against the enemy.

To bring back the Pretender, the Jacobites formed a Scotch and an English and an Irish constitution. The English constitution embraced the Mother Lodge of York and that of London, which latter separated from York, and with a new spring of action started into life as the Grand Lodge of London in 1717. The Jacobite nobles brought it to France chiefly to aid their attempts in favour of the Stuarts. They opened a lodge called the "Amity and Fraternity," in Dunkirk, in 1721, and in 1725 the Lord Derwentwater opened the famous Mother Lodge of Paris. Masonry soon spread to Holland (1730), to Germany in 1736, to Ireland in 1729, and afterwards to Italy, Spain and Europe generally. All its lodges were placed under the Grand Lodge of England, and remained so for many years.

I mention these facts and dates in order to let you see that precisely at the period when Freemasonry was thus extending abroad, the Infidelity, which had been introduced by Bayle and openly advocated by Voltaire, was being disseminated largely amongst the corrupt nobility of France and of Europe generally. It was, as we have already seen, a period of universal licence in morals with the great in every country, and the members of the Grand Lodge in England were generally men of easy virtue whose example was agreeable to Continental libertines.

Voltaire found that the Masonry to which he had been affiliated in London was a capital means of diffusing his doctrines among the courtiers, the men of letters and the public of France. It was like himself, the incarnation of hypocrisy and lying. It came recommended by an appearance of philanthropy and of religion. Ashmole gave it the open Bible, together with the square and compass. It called the world to witness that it believed in God, "the great Architect of the Universe." It had "an open eye," which may be taken for God's all-seeing providence, or for the impossibility of a sworn Mason escaping his fate if he revealed the secrets of the craft or failed to obey the orders he was selected to carry out. It made members known to each other, just as did the ancient craft, in every country, and professed to take charge of the orphans and widows of deceased brethren who could not provide for them. But, in its secret conclaves and in its ascending degrees, it had means to tell the victim whom it could count upon, that the "Architect" meant a circle, a nothing;[3] that the open Bible was the universe; and that the square and compass was simply the fitness of things—the means to make all men "fraternal, equal and free" in some impossible Utopia it promised but never gave. In the recesses of its lodges, the political conspirator found the men and the means to arrive at his ends in security. Those who ambitioned office found there

[3] See section xxi. "Freemasonry with Ourselves," pp. 205-225.

the means of advancement. The old spirit breathed into the fraternity by Socinus, and nourished so well by the heretical libertines of the England and Germany of the seventeenth century, and perfected by the Infidels of the eighteenth, was master in all its lodges. Banquets, ribald songs and jests, revelling in sin, constituted from the beginning a leading feature in its life. Lodges became the secure home for the roue, the spendthrift, the man of broken fortunes, the Infidel, and the depraved of the upper classes. Such attractive centres of sin, therefore, spread over Europe with great rapidity. They were encouraged not only by Voltaire, but by his whole host of Atheistic writers, philosophers, encyclopedists, revolutionists, and rakes. The scoundrels of Europe found congenial employment in them; and before twenty years elapsed from their first introduction the lodges were a power in Europe, formidable by the union which subsisted between them all, and by the wealth, social position, and unscrupulousness of those who formed their brotherhood. The principles fashionable—and indeed alone tolerated—in them all, before long, were the principles of Voltaire and of his school. This led in time to the Union and "Illuminism" of Freemasonry.

V

THE UNION AND "ILLUMINISM" OF FREEMASONRY

WITH the aid of Voltaire, and of his party, Freemasonry rapidly spread amongst the higher classes of France and wherever else in Europe the influence of the French Infidels extended. It soon after obtained immense power of union and propagandism. In France and everywhere else it had an English, a Scotch, and a local obedience. These had separate constitutions and officers, even separate grades, but all were identical in essence and in aim. A brother in one was a brother in all. However, it seemed to the leaders that more unity was needed, and aided by the adhesion of the Duke of Chartres, subsequently better known as the Duke of Orleans, the infamous Philippe-Égalité, who was Grand Master of the Scotch Masonic Body in France, the French Masons in the English obedience desiring independence of the Mother Lodge of England, separated and elected him the first Grand Master of the since celebrated Grand Orient of France. Two years after this, the execrable "Androgyne" lodges for women, called "Lodges of Adoption" were established, and had as Grand Mistress over them all the Duchess of Bourbon, sister of Égalité. The Infidels, by extending these lodges for women, obtained an immense amount of influence, which they otherwise never could attain. They thus invaded the domestic circle of the Court of France and of every Court in Europe. Thus, too, the royal edicts, the decrees of Clement XII and Benedict XIV against Freemasonry, and the efforts of conscientious officers, were rendered completely inoperative. After the death of Voltaire, the extension of Freemasonry became alarming; but no State effort could then stop its progress. It daily grew more powerful and more corrupt. It began already to extend its influence into every department of state. Promotion in the army, in the navy, in the public service, in the law, and even to the fat benefices "in commendam" of the Church, became impossible without its aid;[1] and at

---

[1] Before the celebrated "Convent" of Wilhelmsbad there was a thorough understanding between the Freemasons of the various Catholic countries of Continental Europe. This was manifested in the horrible intrigues which led to the suppression of the Society of Jesus in France, Spain, Portugal, Germany, and Naples; and which finally compelled Clement XIV to dissolve the great body by ecclesiastical authority. No doubt the Jesuits had very potent enemies in the Jansenists, the Gallicans, and in others whose party spirit and jealousy were stronger than their sense of the real good

this precise juncture, when the political fortunes of France were, for many reasons, growing desperate, two events occurred to make the already general and

of religion. But without the unscrupulous intrigues of the Infidels of Voltaire's school banded into a compact active league by the newly-developed Freemasonry, the influence of the sects of Christians hostile to the Order could never effect an effacement so complete and so general. Anglican lodges, we must remember, appeared in Spain and Portugal as soon as in France. One was opened in Gibraltar in 1726, and one in Madrid in 1727. This latter broke with the mother lodge of London in 1779, and founded lodges in Barcelona, Cadiz, Vallidolid, and other cities. There were several lodges at work in Lisbon as early as 1735. The Duke of Choiseul, a Freemason, with the aid of the abominable de Pompadour, the harlot of the still more abominable Louis XV, succeeded in driving the Jesuits from France. He then set about influencing his brother Masons, the Count De Aranda, Prime Minister of Charles III of Spain, and the infamous Carvalho-Pombal, the alter ego of the weak King of Portugal, to do the same work in the Catholic States of their respective sovereigns. The Marquis de L'Angle, a French Freemason Atheist, and friend of Choiseul, thus writes of De Aranda—"He is the only man of which Spain can be proud of at this moment. He is the sole Spaniard of our days whom posterity will place on its tablets. It is he whom it will love to place on the front of all its temples, and whose name it will engrave on its escutcheon together with the names of Luther, of Calvin, of Mahomet, of William Penn, and of Jesus Christ! It is he who desired to sell the wardrobe of the saints, the property of virgins, and to convert the cross, the chandeliers, the patens, &c., into bridges and inns and main roads." We cannot be surprised at what De Aranda attempted after this testimony. He conspired with Choiseul to forge a letter as if from the General of the Jesuits, Ricci, which purported to prove that the King's mother was an adulteress, and that the King had no claim to the Spanish throne. Secretly, therefore, an order was obtained from the weak Monarch, and on a given day and hour the Jesuits in all parts of the Spanish dominions were dragged from their homes, placed on board ships, and cast on the shores of the Pontifical States in a condition of utter destitution. A calumny as atrocious and unfounded enabled Pombal to inflict a worse fate on the Jesuits of Portugal and its dependencies.

corrupt Freemasonry still more formidable. These were the advent of the Illuminism of Saint Martin in France, and that of Adam Weishaupt in Germany, and the increased corruption introduced principally by means of women-Freemasons.

A Portuguese Jew, named Martinez Pasqualis, was the first to introduce Illuminism into the Lodge of Lyons, and his system was afterwards perfected in wickedness by Saint Martin, from whom French Illuminism took its name. Illuminism meant the extreme extent of immorality, Atheism, anarchy, levelling, and bloodshed, to which the principles of Masonry could be carried. It meant a universal conspiracy against the Church and established order. It constituted a degree of advancement for all the lodges, and powerfully aided to make them the centres of revolutionary intrigue and of political manipulation which they soon became in the hands of men at once sunk in Atheism and moral corruption.

An idea of these lodges may be obtained from a description given of that of Ermanonville, by M. Le Marquis de Lefroi, in *Dictionnaire des Erreurs Sociétés*, quoted by Deschamps, vol. ii, page 93.

"It is known," he says, "that the Chateau de Ermanonville belonging to the Sieur Girardin, about ten leagues from Paris, was a famous haunt of Illuminism. It is known that there, near the tomb of

Jean-Jacques, under the pretext of bringing men back to the age of nature, reigned the most horrible dissoluteness of morals. Nothing can equal the turpitude of morals which reigns amongst that horde of Ermanonville. Every woman admitted to the mysteries became common to the brothers, and was delivered up to the chance or to the choice of these true 'Adamites.'" Barruel in his *Memoires sur le Jacobinisme*, vol. iv. p. 334, says "that M. Leseure, the father of the hero of La Vendée, having been affiliated to a lodge of this kind, and having, in obedience to the promptings of conscience, abandoned it, was soon after poisoned." He himself declared to the Marquis de Montron that he fell a victim to "that infamous horde of the Illuminati."

The Illuminism of Saint Martin was simply an advance in the intensity of immorality, Atheism, secrecy, and terror, which already reigned in the lodges of France. It planned a deeper means of revolution and destruction. It became in its hidden depths a lair in which the Atheists of the period could mature their plans for the overthrow of the existing order of things to their own best advantage. It gave itself very captivating names. Its members were "Knights of Beneficence," "Good Templars," "Knights of St. John," &c. They numbered, however, amongst them, the most active, daring, and unscrupulous members of

Masonry. They set themselves at work to dominate over and to control the entire body. They had no system, any more than any other sort of Masons, to give the world instead of that which they determined to pull down. The state of nature, goods and the sexes in common, no God, and instead of God a hatred for everything sustaining the idea of God, formed about the sum total of the happiness which they desired to see reign in a world where people should be reduced to a level resembling that of wild cattle in the American prairies. This was the Illumination they destined for humanity; yet such was the infatuation inspired by their immoral and strange doctrines that nobles, princes, and monarchs of the period, including Frederick II of Prussia and the silly Joseph II of Austria, admitted to a part of their secrets, were the tools and the dupes, and even the accomplices, of these infamous conspirators.

VI

THE ILLUMINISM OF ADAM WEISHAUPT

BUT the Illuminism of Lyons was destined soon to have a world-wide and ineradicable hold on the Masonry of the world by means of an adept far more able than Saint Martin or any of his associates. This was Adam Weishaupt, a Professor of Canon Law in the University of Munich. I shall detain you a while to consider this remarkable individual who, more than any of the Atheists that have arisen in Masonry, has been the cause of the success of its agencies in controlling the fate of the world since his day. Had Weishaupt not lived, Masonry may have ceased to be a power after the reaction consequent on the first French Revolution. He gave it a form and character which caused it to outlive that reaction, to energize it to the present day, and which will cause it to advance until its final conflict with Christianity must determine whether Christ or Satan shall reign on this earth to the end.

Voltaire's will to do God and man injury was as strong as that of Weishaupt. His disciples, D'Alembert, Diderot, Damilaville, Condorcet, and the rest, were as fully determined as he was, to eradicate Christianity. But they desired in its stead a system with only a mitigated antipathy for monarchy, and which might have tolerated for a long time such kings as Frederick of Prussia, and such Empresses as Catherine of Russia. But the hatred for God and all form of worship, and the determination to found a universal republic on the lines of Communism, was on the part of Weishaupt a settled sentiment. Possessed of a rare power of organization, an education in law which made him a pre-eminent teacher in its highest faculty, an extended knowledge of men and things, a command over himself, a repute for external morality, and finally, a position calculated to win able disciples, Weishaupt employed for fifty years after the death of Voltaire, his whole life and energies in the one work of perfecting secret associations to accomplish by deep deceit, and by force when that should be practical, the ruin of the existing order of religion, civilization, and government, in order to plant in its stead his own system of Atheism and Socialism.

He found contemporary Masonry well adapted for his ends. His object was to extend it as far as possible as a means of seducing men away from Christianity. He well knew that Masonry and the Church were in mortal conflict, and that the moment a man became a Mason, he, that instant, became excommunicated; he lost the grace of God; he passed into a state of hostility to the Church; he ceased to approach the Sacraments; he was constituted in a state of rebellion; he forfeited his liberty to unknown superiors; he took a dreadful oath—perhaps many— not to reveal the secrets then, or at any after time, to be committed to his keeping; and finally, he placed himself amongst men, all of whom were in his own position, and in whose society it was possible and easy for the astute disciples of Weishaupt to lead him farther on the road to ruin.

Weishaupt's view, then, was first to entice men into Masonry—into the lowest degree. A great gain for evil was thus at once obtained. But a man, though in Masonry, may not be willing to become an Atheist and a Socialist, for some time at least. He may have in his heart a profound conviction that a God existed, and some hope left of returning to that God at or before his death. He may have entered Masonry for purposes of ambition, for motives of vanity, from mere lightness of character. He may continue his prayers, and refuse, if a Catholic, to give up the Mother of God and some practice of piety loved by him from his youth. But Masonry was a capital system to wean a man gradually away from all these things. It did not at once deny the existence of God, nor at once attack the Christian Dispensation. It commenced by giving the Christian idea of God, an easy, and, under semblance of respect, an almost imperceptible shake. It swore by the name of God in all its oaths. It called him, however, not a Creator, only an architect—the great Architect of the universe. It carefully avoided all mention of Christ, of the Adorable Trinity, of the Unity of the Faith, or of any faith. It protested a respect for the convictions of every man, for the idolatrous Parsee, for the Mahommedan, for the Heretic, the Schismatic, the Catholic. By-and-by, it gave, in higher degrees, a ruder shock to the belief in the Deity and a gradual inducement to favour Naturalism. This it did gradually, imperceptibly, but effectually. Now, to a man who meditated the vast designs of social and religious destruction contemplated by Weishaupt, Masonry, especially the Masonry of his period, was the most effective means that could be conceived. In its midst, therefore, he planted his disciples, well versed in his system. These consisted of three classes, each class having subdivisions, and all of which were high degrees of Masonry. The first class of Illuminati, was that of preparation. It consisted of two degrees, namely, the degree of Novice and that of Minerval. The Minervals formed the great body of the order, and were under the direction of certain chiefs, who themselves were subjected to other agencies invisible to those instructed by themselves. Weishaupt instructed the teachers of the Minervals to propose each year to their scholars some interesting questions, to cause them to write themes calculated to spread impiety amongst the people, such as burlesques on the Psalms, pasquinades on the Prophets, and caricatures of personages of the Old Testament after the manner of Voltaire and his school. It is surprising with what exactitude these Minervals follow out the instructions of Weishaupt to this day. At this moment, in London, under the eyes of the Lord Chancellor, pamphlets, with hideous woodcuts, ridiculing David, "the man after God's own heart," are weekly published. One of these, which was handed to me in a public place, had a woodcut representing the "meek Monarch of Judea," with a head just severed from a human body in one hand, and the sword that did the deed in the other. Another represented him amidst a set of ridiculous figures dancing. From this we can easily judge that illuminated Masonry is at work somewhere even in London, and that the Masonry in high quarters is blind to its excesses, exactly as happened in France a few years before the French Revolution. Now these Minervals, if they manifested what the German Masons called "religionary" inclinations, might indeed receive the first three Masonic degrees, but they were not to be further promoted in Illuminism. They were relegated to the rank and file of Masonry, who were of use in many ways for the movement, but they were never to be trusted with the real secret. The teacher, without seeming to do so, was ordered to encourage, but not to applaud publicly, such blasphemies as the Minervals might make use of in their essays. They were to be led on, seemingly by themselves, in the ways of irreligion, immorality, and Atheism, until ripe for further promotion in evil progress. Finally, in the advanced grades of Illuminated Major and Minor, and in those of Scotch Knight and Epopte or Priest they were told the whole secret of the Order as follows, in a discourse by the initiator.

"Remember," he said, "that from the first invitations which we have given you, in order to attract you to us, we have commenced by telling you that in the projects of our Order there did not enter any designs against religion. You remember that such an assurance was again given to you when you were admitted into the ranks of our novices, and that it was repeated when you entered into our Minerval

Academy. Remember also how much from the first grades we have spoken to you of morality and virtue, but at the same time how much the studies which we prescribed for you and the instructions which we gave you rendered both morality and virtue independent of all religion; how much we have been at pains to make you understand, while making to you the eulogy of religion, that it was not anything else than those mysteries, and that worship degenerated in the hands of the priest. You remember with what art, with what simulated respect, we have spoken to you of Christ and of his Gospel; but in the grades of greater Illuminism, of Scotch Knight, and of Epopte or Priest, how we have known to form from Christ's Gospel that of our reason, and from its morality that of nature, and from its religion that of nature, and from religion, reason, morality, and nature, to make the religion, and the morality of the rights of man, of equality, and of liberty. Remember that while insinuating to you the different parts of this system, we have caused them to bud forth from yourselves as if your own opinions. We have placed you on the way; you have replied to our questions very much more than we did to yours. When we demanded of you, for example, whether the religions of peoples responded to the end for which men adopted them; if the religion of Christ, pure and simple, was that which the different Sects professed to-day, we know well enough what to hold. But it was necessary to knew to what point we had succeeded to cause our sentiments to germinate in you. We have had very many prejudices to overcome in you, before being able to persuade you that the pretended religion of Christ was nothing else than the work of priests, of imposture, and of tyranny. If it be so with that religion so much proclaimed and admired, what are we to think of other religions? Understand, then, that they have all the same fictions for their origin, that they are all equally founded on lying, error, chimera, and imposture. Behold our secret!

"The turns and counter-turns which it was necessary to make; the eulogies which it was necessary to give to the pretended secret schools; the fable of the Freemasons being in possession of the veritable doctrine; and our Illuminism to-day, the sole inheritor of these mysteries, will no longer astonish you at this moment. If, in order to destroy all Christianity, all religion, we have pretended to have the sole true religion, remember that the end justifies the means, and that the wise ought to take all the means to do good, which the wicked take to do evil. Those which we have taken to deliver you, those which we take to deliver one day the human race from all religion, are nothing else than a pious fraud which we reserve to unveil some day in the grade of Magus or Philosopher Illuminated."—Ségur: *Le Secret de la Franc-Maçonnerie*, p. 49.

The above extract will serve to show you what manner of man Weishaupt was, and the quality of the teaching he invented. His organization— for the perfection of which he deeply studied the constitution of the then suppressed Society of Jesus—contemplated placing the thread of the whole conspiracy, destined to be controlled by the Illuminati, in the hands of one man, advised by a small council. The Illuminati were to be in Masonry and of Masonry, so as to move amongst its members secretly. They were so trained that they could obtain the mastery in every form of secret society, and thus render it subservient to their own Chief. Their fidelity to him was made perfect by the most severe and complex system of espionage. The Chief himself was kept safe by his position, his long training, and by his council. It thus happened that no matter to what office or position the Illuminati attained, they had to become subservient to the general aims of the Order. Weishaupt, after being deprived of his professorship in Bavaria, found an asylum with the Prince of Coburg Gotha, where he remained in honour, affluence and security, until his death in 1830. He continued all his life the Chief of the Illuminati, and this fact may account, in large measure, for the fidelity with which the Illuminati of the Revolution, the Directory, Consulate, the Empire, the Restoration, and the Revolution of 1830, invariably earned out his programme of perpetual conspiracy for the ends he had in view. It may also account for the strange vitality of the spirit of the Illuminati in Italy, Switzerland, Germany, and Spain, and of its continuance through the "Illuminated" reigns of Nubius and Palmerston, the successors of Weishaupt to our own day. This we shall see further on; but, meanwhile, we shall glance at the first step of Weishaupt to rule over Masonry through his disciples. This was by calling together the famous "General Council" of Freemasonry, known as the Convent of Wilhelmsbad.

VII

THE CONVENT OF WILHELMSBAD

From its rise Freemasonry appears as a kind of dark parody of the Church of Christ. The names taken by its dignitaries, the form of its hierarchy, the designations affected by its lodges and "obediences," the language of its rituals, all seem to be a kind of aping after the usages of Christianity. When Saint Martin wished to spread his Illuminism in France, he managed to have a meeting of deputy Masons from all the lodges in that country. This was designated the "Convent of the Gauls;" and Lyons, the place of its meeting, was called "The Holy City." Weishaupt had more extended views. He meant to reach all humanity by means of Masonry, and looked for a "Convent" far more general than that of Lyons. When, therefore, he had matured his plans for impregnating the Masonry of the world with his infernal system, he began to cast about for means to call that Convent. The Illuminism of Saint Martin was in full sympathy with him, but it could not effect his purpose. He wanted a kind of General Council of the Masonry extended at the time throughout the earth to be called together; and he hoped that, by adroitly manipulating the representatives whom he knew would be sent to it by the lodges of every nationality of Masons, his own Illuminism might be adopted as a kind of high, arch, or hidden, Masonry, throughout its entire extent. He succeeded in his design, and in 1781, under the official convocation of the Duke of Brunswick, acting as Supreme Grand Master, deputies from every country where Freemasonry existed were summoned to meet at Wilhelmsbad in council. They came from every portion of the British Empire; from the newly formed United States of America; from all the Nations of Continental Europe, every one of which, at that period, had lodges; from the territories of the Grand Turk, and from the Indian and Colonial possessions of France, Spain, Portugal, and Holland. The principal and most numerous representatives were, however, from Germany and France. Through the skilful agency of the notorious Baron Knigge, and another still more astute adept of his, named Dittfort, Weishaupt completely controlled this Council. He further caused measures to be there concerted which in a few years led to the French Revolution, and afterwards handed Germany over to the French revolutionary Generals acting under the Girondins, the Jacobins, and the Directory. I would wish, if time permitted, to enter at length into the proofs of this fact. It will suffice, however, for my present purpose, to state that more than sufficient evidence of it was found by the Bavarian Government, which had, some five years later, to suppress the Illuminati, and that one of the members of the convent, the Count de Virene, was struck with such horror at the depravity of the body that he abandoned Illuminism and became a fervent Catholic. He said to a friend:—"I will not tell you the secrets which I bring, but I can say that a conspiracy is laid so secret and so deep that it will be very difficult for monarchy and religion not to succomb to it." It may be also of use to remark that many of the leaders of the French Revolution, and notably most of those who lived through it, and profited by it, were deputy Masons sent from various lodges in France to the Convent of Wilhelmsbad.

VIII

CABALISTIC MASONRY OR MASONIC SPIRITISM

BEFORE proceeding further with the history of Freemasonry, I shall stay a moment to consider a very remarkable feature in its strange composition, without which it scarcely ever appears. The world was never without wizards, witches, necromancers, jugglers, and those who really had, or through imposture, pretended to have, intercourse with demons. Masonry in its various ramifications is the great continuator of this feature of a past which we had thought departed for ever. Spirit-rapping, table-turning, medium-imposture, etc., distinguish its adepts in Protestant countries and in Catholic ones. We have almost incredible stories of the intercourse with the devil and his angels, which men like the Carbonari of Italy maintain. However, from the very beginning Freemasonry has had a kind of peculiar dark mysticism connected with it. It loves to revel in such mysteries as the secret conclaves that the Jews used to practise in the countries in which they were persecuted, and which were common among those unclean heretics, the Bulgarians, the Gnostics, the Albigenses, and the Waldenses. The excesses alleged against the Templars were also accompanied by secret signs and symbols which Masonry adopted. But whatever may have been the extent of this mysticism in Masonry before, a spurious kind of spiritism became part of its very essence since the advent of the celebrated Cagliostro, who travelled all over Europe under the instructions of Weishaupt, and founded more lodges than did any individual Freemason then or since. The real name of this arch-imposter was Balsamo. He was an inveterate sorcerer, and in his peregrinations in the East, picked up from every source the secrets of alchemy, astrology, jugglery, legerdemain, and occult science of every kind about which he could get any information. Like the Masonry to which he became affiliated at an early period, he was an adept at acting and speaking a lie. He suited Weishaupt, who, though knowing him to be an imposter, nevertheless employed for him the diffusion of Illuminism. Accompanied by his no less celebrated wife, Lorenza, he appeared in Venice as the Marquis Pelligrini, and subsequently traversed Italy, Germany, Spain, England, the Netherlands, and Russia. In the latter country he amassed, at the Court of Catherine II, an immense fortune. In France, assisted by the efforts of the Illuminati, he was received as a kind of demigod, and called the divine Cagliostro. He established new lodges in all parts of the country. At Bordeaux he remained eleven months for this purpose. In Paris he established lodges for women of a peculiarly cabalistic and impure kind, with inner departments horribly mysterious. At the reception of members he used rites and ceremonies exactly resembling the absurd practices of spirit mediums, who see and speak to spirits, etc., and introduced all that nonsense with which we are made now familiar by his modern followers. He claimed the power of conferring immortal youth, health, and beauty, and what he called moral and physical regeneration, by the aid of drugs and Illuminated Masonry. He was the father and the founder of the existing rite of Misraim—the Egyptian rite in Masonry. The scoundrel became involved in the celebrated case of the "Diamond Necklace," and was sent to the Bastille, from which he managed to pass to England, where, in 1787, he undertook to foretell the destruction of the Bastille, and of the Monarchy of France, the Revolution, and—but here he miscalculated— the advent of a Prince who would abolish Lettres de Cachet, convoke the States General, and establish the worship of Reason. All these measures were resolved on at Wilhelmsbad, and Cagliostro of course knew that well. His only miscalculation was regarding the Prince Grand Master. The Revolution went on a little too far for the wretched Égalité, who ended his treason to his house by losing his head at the guillotine. As to Cagliostro, he made his way to Rome, where the Inquisition put an end to his exploits on detecting his attempts at Illuminism. His secret powers could not deliver him from prison. He died there miserably, in 1795, after attempting to strangle a poor Capuchin whom he asked for as a confessor, and in whose habit he had hoped to escape. This impostor is of course made a martyr to the Inquisition accordingly. Masonry does much to disown Cagliostro; but with a strange inconsistency it keeps the Egyptian rite founded by him, and clings to mysticism of the debased kind he introduced. It is wonderful how extremes thus meet,— how men who make it a sign of intellectual strength to deny the existence of the God that made them bow down stupidly and superstitiously before devils, real or imaginary. Necromancy is a characteristic of Antichrist, of whom we read, "that he will show great signs and wonders so as to deceive, if that were possible, even the elect." He will be when, he comes both a Cromwell and a Cagliostro.

IX

THE FRENCH REVOLUTION

I MAY here remark that the conspiracy of the Illuminati, and of Freemasonry generally, was far from being a secret to many of the Courts of Europe. But, then, just as at the present moment, it had friends, female as well as male, in every court. These baulked the wholesome attempts of some rulers to stay its deadly intrigues against princes, governments, and all order, as well as against its one grand enemy, the Church of Jesus Christ. The Court of Bavaria found out, as I have said, but only by an accident, a part of the plans of the Illuminati, and gave the alarm; but, strange to say, that alarm was unheeded by the other Courts of Europe, Catholic as well as Protestant. A Revolution was expected, but, as now, each Court hoped to stave off the worst consequences from itself, and to profit by the ruin of its neighbours. The voice of the Holy Father was raised against Freemasonry again and again. Clement VIII, Benedict XIV, and other Pontiffs, condemned it. The Agents and

Ministers of the Holy See, gave private advices and made urgent appeals to have the evil stopped while yet the powers of Europe could do so. These were all baffled, and the Court of the Grand Monarch and every Court of Continental Europe slept in the torpor of a living death, until wakened to a true sense of danger at a period far too late to remedy the disasters which irreligion, vice, stupidity, and recklessness hastened. The lodges of the Illuminati in France meanwhile carried on the conspiracy. They had amassed and expended immense sums in deluging the country with immoral and Atheistic literature.

Mirabeau, in his *Monarchic Prussienne* (vol. 6, page 67), published before the Revolution, thus speaks of these sums:—

"Masonry in general, and especially the branch of the Templars, produced annually immense sums by means of the cost of receptions and contributions of every kind. A part of the total was employed in the expenses of the order, but another part, much more considerable, went into a general fund, of which no one, except the first amongst the brethren, knew the destination," Cagliostro, when questioned before the Holy Roman Inquisition, "confessed that he led his sumptuous existence thanks to the funds furnished him by the Illuminati. He also stated that he had a commission from Weishaupt to prepare the French Lodges to receive his direction."— See Deschamps, v., p. 129.

Discontent was thus sown broadcast amongst every class of the population. Masonic Lodges multiplied, inspired by the instructed emissaries of the remorseless Weishaupt; and the direct work of Freemasonry in subsequent events is manifest not only in the detailed prophecy of Cagliostro, founded on what he knew was decided upon; but is still more clearly evidenced by a second convent, held by the French Illuminati, where everything was arranged for the Revolution. The men prominent in this conclave were the men subsequently most active in every scene that followed. Mirabeau, Lafayette, Fouché, Talleyrand, Danton, Murat, Robespierre, Cambaceres, and in fact every foremost name in the subsequent convulsions of the country were not only Illuminati, but foremost amongst the Illuminati.[1]

[1] It is commonly believed that the encyclopædists and philosophers were the only men who overturned by their writings altar and throne at the time of the Revolution. But, apart from the facts that these writers were to a man Freemasons, and the most daring and plotting of Freemasons, we have abundant authority to prove that other Freemasons were everywhere even more practically engaged in the same work. Louis Blanc, who will be accepted as an authority on this point, thus writes:— "It is of consequence to introduce the reader into the mine which at that time was being dug beneath thrones and altars by revolutionists, very much more profound and active than the encyclopædists: an association composed of men of all countries, of all religions,

Some disappeared under their own guillotine; others outlived the doom of their fellows. Constantly, the men of the whole conspiracy had understandings and relations with each other. Weishaupt, at the safe distance of Coburg-Gotha, gave them his willing aid and that of the German Freemasons. This concert enabled them to float on every billow which the troubled sea of the Revolution caused to swell; and if they did not succeed in making France and all Eu-

of all ranks, bound together by symbolic bonds, engaged under an inviolable oath to preserve the secret of their interior existence. They were forced to undergo terrific proofs while occupying themselves with fantastic ceremonies, but otherwise practised beneficence and looked upon themselves as equals though divided in three classes, apprentices, companions, and masters. Freemasonry consists in that. Now, on the eve of the French Revolution, Freemasonry was found to have received an immense development. Spread throughout the whole of Europe, it seconded the meditative genius of Germany, agitated France silently, and presented everywhere the image of a society founded on principles contrary to those of civil society." Mgr. Ségur writes on this:—"See to what a point the reign of Jesus Christ was menaced at the hour the Revolution broke out. It was not France alone that it agitated, but the whole of Europe. What do I say? The world was in the power of Masonry. All the lodges of the world came in 1781 to Wilhelmsbad by delegates from Europe, Asia, Africa and America; from the most distant coasts discovered by navigators, they came, zealous apostles of Masonry ... They all returned penetrated with the Illuminism of Weishaupt, that is Atheism, and animated with the poison of incredulity with which the orators of the Convent had inspired them. Europe and the Masonic world were then in arms against Catholicism. Therefore, when the signal was given, the shock was terrible, terrible especially in France, in Italy, in Spain, in the Catholic nations which they wished to separate from the Pope and cast into schism, until the time came when they would completely de-Christianize them. This accounts well for the captivities of Pius VI and Pius VII."

rope a social ruin, such as that contemplated at Wilhelmsbad, it was from want of power, not from want of will. Position and wealth made many of them desire to conserve what the Revolution threw into their hands. But they remained under all changes of fortune Freemasons, as they and their successors are to this day. Perhaps, under the influence of oaths, of secret terror, and of the Sect, they dare not remain long otherwise. One or two individuals may drop aside; but some fatality or necessity keeps the leaders Illuminati always. They as a whole body remain ever the same, and recoil before political adversity, only to gather more strength for a future attack upon religion and order still wider and more fatal than the one which preceded it. They are not at any time one whit less determined to plunge the world into the anarchy and bloodshed they created at the French Revolution, than they were in 1789. On this point let one of themselves speak:—(Extracts from *Proofs of a Conspiracy*, by John Robison, A.M., Professor of Natural Philosophy and Secretary to the Royal Society of Edinburgh— The Third Edition, corrected, 1789.)

"I have been able to trace these attempts, made, through a course of fifty years, under the specious pretext of enlightening the world by the torch of philosophy, and of dispelling the clouds of civil and religious superstition which keep the nations of Europe in darkness and slavery. I have observed these doctrines gradually diffusing and mixing with all the different systems of Free Masonry; till, at last, AN ASSOCIATION HAS been formed for the express purpose of rooting OUT ALL THE RELIGIOUS ESTABLISHMENTS, AND OVERTURNING ALL THE EXISTING GOVERNMENTS OF EUROPE. I have Seen this Association exerting itself zealously and systematically, till it has become almost irresistible: and I have seen that the most active leaders in the French Revolution were members of this Association, and conducted their first movements according to its principles, and by means of its instructions and assistance, formally requested and obtained: lastly, I have seen that this Association still exists, still works in secret, and that not only several appearances among ourselves show that its emissaries are endeavouring to propagate their detestable doctrines among us, but that the Association has Lodges in Britain corresponding with the mother Lodge at Munich ever since 1784.

"If all this were a matter of mere curiosity, and susceptible of no good use, it would have been better to have kept it to myself than to disturb my neighbours with the knowledge of a state of things which they cannot amend. But if it shall appear that the minds of my countrymen are misled in the very same manner as were those of our continental neighbours—if I can show that the reasonings which make a very strong impression on some persons in this country are the same which actually produced the dangerous association in Germany; and that they had this unhappy influence solely because they were thought to be sincere, and the expressions of the sentiments of the speakers. If I can show that this was all a cheat, and that the Leaders of this Association disbelieved every word that they uttered, and every doctrine that they taught; and that their real intention was to abolish all religion, overturn every government, and make the world a general plunder and a wreck ... I cannot but think that such information will make my countrymen hesitate a little, and receive with caution, and even distrust, addresses and instructions which flatter our self-conceit."—(pp. 11-13.)

These words of Robison show, that as early as 1797, the connection between Freemasonry and the French Revolution was well understood. Since then Louis Blanc, and other Masonic writers, have gloried in the fact. "Our end," said the celebrated Alta Vendita, to which I shall have to refer presently, "is that of Voltaire and the French Revolution." In fact, what Freemasonry did in France, it now labours, with greater caution, to effect on some future day throughout the entire world. It then submitted, with perfect docility, to a great military leader, who arose out of its own work and principles. Such another leader will finally direct its last efforts against God and man. That leader will be Antichrist.

X

NAPOLEON AND FREEMASONRY

THE leader who arose out of the first French Revolution, and whose military and diplomatic fame is still fresh in the recollection of many of the present generation—that leader was Napoleon Bonaparte. In the days of his greatest prosperity, nothing was so distasteful to him as to be reminded of his Jacobin past. He then wished to pose as another Charlemagne, or Rudolph of Hapsburg. He wished to be considered the friend of religion, and of the Catholic religion in particular. He did something for the restoration of the Church in France, but it was as little as he could help. It, perhaps, prevented a more wholesome and complete reaction in favour of the true religious aspirations of the population. It was done grudgingly, parsimoniously, and meanly. And when it had been done, Napoleon did all he could to undo its benefits. He soon became the persecutor—the heartless, cruel, ungrateful persecutor of the Pontiff, and an opponent to the best interests of religion in France, and in every country which had the misfortune to fall under his sway. The reason for all this was, that Napoleon had commenced his career as a Freemason, and a Freemason he remained in spirit and in effect to the end of his life. It is known that he owed his first elevation to the Jacobins, and that his earliest patron was Robespierre. His first campaign in Italy was characterized by the utmost brutality which could gratify Masonic hatred for the Church. He suppressed the abodes of the consecrated servants of God, sacked churches, cathedrals, and sanctuaries, and reduced the Pope to the direst extremities. His language was the reflex of his acts and of his heart. His letters breathe everywhere the spirit of advanced Freemasonry, gloating over the wounds it had been able to inflict upon the Spouse of Christ. Yet this adventurer has, with great adroitness, been able to pass with many, and especially in Ireland, as a good Catholic. Because he was the enemy of England, or rather that England led by the counsels of Pitt and Burke, constituted herself the implacable enemy of the Revolution of which he was the incarnation and continuation, many opposed to England for political reasons, regard Bonaparte as a kind of hero. No one can doubt the military genius of the man, nor indeed his great general ability; but he was in all his acts what Freemasonry made him. He was mean, selfish, tyrannical, cruel. He was reckless of blood. He could tolerate or use the Church while that suited his policy. But he had from the beginning to the very end of his career that thorough indifference to her welfare, and want of belief in her doctrines, which an early and life-long connection with the Illuminati inspired.

Father Deschamps writes of him: "Napoleon Bonaparte was in effect an advanced Freemason, and his reign has been the most flourishing epoch of Freemasonry. During the reign of terror the Grand Orient ceased its activity. The moment Napoleon seized power the lodges were opened in every place."

I have said that the revolutionary rulers in France were all Illuminati—that is Freemasons of the most pronounced type—whose ultimate aim was the destruction of every existing religion and form of secular government, in order to found an atheistic, social republic, which would extend throughout the world and embrace all mankind. Freemasonry welcomes, as we have seen, the Mahommedan, the Indian, the Chinese, and the Buddhist, as well as the Christian and the Jew. It designs to conquer all, as a means of bringing all into the one level of Atheism and Communism. When, therefore, its Directory, in their desire to get rid of Napoleon, planned the expedition to Egypt and Asia, they meant the realization of a part of this programme, as well as the removal of a troublesome rival. A universal monarchy is, in their idea, the most efficacious means for arriving at a universal republic. Once obtained, the dagger with which they removed Gustavus III of Sweden, or the guillotine by which they rid France of Louis XVI, can at any moment remove Caesar and call in Brutus. They are not the men to recoil before deeds of blood for the accomplishment of their purposes.

Now Napoleon, who was, as Father Deschamps informs us, a member of the lodge of the Templars, the extreme Illuminated lodge of Lyons, and had given proof of his fidelity to Masonry in Italy, was the very man to extend the rule of Republicanism throughout Asia. He appeared in Egypt with the same professions of hypocritical respect for the Koran, the Prophet, and Mahommedanism, as he afterwards made when it suited his policy for Catholicism. His address to the people of Egypt will prove this. It ran as follows, with true Masonic hypocrisy:—

"Cadis, Chieks, Imans, tell the people that we are the friends of true Mussulmen; that we respect more than the Mamelukes do, God, His Prophet, and the Alkoran. Is it not we who have destroyed the Pope, who wished that war should be made against the Mussulman? Is it not we who have destroyed the Knights of Malta, because these madmen thought that God willed them to make war upon the Mussulman? Is it not we who have been, in all ages the friends of the Grand Seigneur—may God fulfil his desires—and the enemy of his enemies. God is God, and Mahomet is his Prophet! Fear nothing above all for the religion of the Prophet, which I love."

The cool hypocrisy of this address is manifested by a proclamation he made on that occasion to his own soldiers. The same proclamation also shows the value we may place on his protestations of attachment to, and respect for, the usages of Christianity. The following is a translation of it:—

"Soldiers! the peoples with whom we are about to live are Mahommedan. The first article of their faith is this: 'There is no God but God, and Mahomet is his Prophet.' Do not contradict them. Act with them as you have acted with the Jews and with the Italians. Have the same respect for their Muftis and their Imans, as you have had for Rabbis and Bishops. Have for the ceremonies prescribed by the Alkoran, for the Mosques, the same tolerance you had for Convents, for Synagogues, and for the religion of Moses and of Jesus Christ."

We read in the correspondence of Napoleon I, published by order of Napoleon III (vol. v., pp. 185, 191, 241), what he thought of this proclamation at the very end of his career:—

"After all, it was not impossible that circumstances might have brought me to embrace Islam," he said at St. Helena. "Could it be thought that the Empire of the East, and perhaps the subjection of the whole of Asia, was not worth a turban and pantaloons, for it was reduced to so much solely. We would lose only our breeches and our hats. I say that the army, disposed as it was, would have lent itself to that project undoubtedly, and it saw in it nothing but a subject for laughter and pleasantry. Meanwhile, you see the consequences. I took Europe by a back stroke. The old civilization was beaten down, and who then thought to disturb the destinies of our France and the regeneration of the world? Who had dared to undertake it? Who could have accomplished it?"

Neither prosperity nor adversity changed Napoleon. He was a sceptic to the end. He said at St. Helena to Las Cases:

"Everything proclaims the existence of a God—that is not to be doubted—but all our religions are evidently the children of men.

"Why do these religions cry down one another, combat one another? Why has that been in all ages, and all places? It is because men are always men. It is because the Priests have always insinuated, slipped in lies and fraud everywhere.

"Nevertheless," he continued, "from the moment that I had the power, I had been eager to re-establish religion. I used it as the base and the root. It was in my eyes the support of good morality, of true principles, of good manners.

"I am assuredly far from being an Atheist; but I cannot believe all that they teach me in spite of my reason, under penalty of being deceitful and hypocritical.

"To say whence I come, what I am, where I go, is above ray ideas. And nevertheless all that is, I am the watch which exists and does not know itself.

"No doubt," he commented, "but my spirit of mere doubt was, in my quality of Emperor, a benefit for the people Otherwise how could I equally favour sects so contrary, if I had been dominated over by one alone? How could I preserve the independence of my thoughts and of my movements under the suggestions of a confessor who could govern me by means of the fear of hell.

"What an empire could not a wicked man, the most stupid of men, under that title of confessor, exercise over those who govern nations?

"I was so penetrated with these truths that I preserved myself well to act in such a manner, that, in as far as it lay in me, I would educate my son in the same religious lines in which I found myself."

Two months later the ex-Emperor said that from the age of thirteen he had lost all religious faith.

Thiers (*Histoire du Consulat et de l'Empire*, iv. p. 14), says that when Napoleon intended to proclaim himself Emperor, he wished to give the Masons a pledge of his principles, and that he did this by killing the Duke d'Enghien. Ele said, "They wish to destroy the Revolution in attacking it in my person. I will defend it, for I am the Revolution. I, myself—I, myself. They will so consider it from this day forward, for they will know of what we are capable."

A less brave but still more accomplished relative of his, Napoleon III in his *Idées Napoléoniennes*, says:—

"The Revolution dying, but not vanquished, left to Napoleon the accomplishments of its last designs. Enlighten the nations it would have said to him. Place upon solid bases the principal result of our efforts. Execute in extent that which I have done in depth. Be for Europe what I have been for France. That grand mission Napoleon accomplished even to the end."

When Napoleon obtained power, it was we know principally by means of the Illuminated Free-

mason Talleyrand.[1] By him and his confederates of
the Illuminati, he was recalled from. Egypt and
placed in the way of its attainment. His brothers
were—every one of them—deep in the secrets of
the Sect. Its supreme hidden directory saw that a
reaction had set in, which if not averted, would
speedily lead to the return of the exiled Bourbons,
and to the disgorgement of ill-gotten goods on the
part of the revolutionists. As a lesser evil, therefore,
and as a means of forwarding the unification of
Europe which they had planned, by his conquests,
they placed supreme power in the hands of Bonaparte, and urged him on in his career, watching, at

[1] Alexander Dumas in his *Memoires de Garibaldi*, first series, p. 34, tells us:—

"Illuminism and Freemasonry, these two great enemies of royalty, and the adopted
device of both of which was L. P. D., *lilia pedibus destrue*, had a grand part in the French
Revolution.

"Napoleon took Masonry under his protection. Joseph Napoleon was Grand Master of the Order, Joachim Murat second Master adjoint. The Empress Josephine being
at Strasbourg, in 1805, presided over the fete for the adoption of the lodge of True
Chevaliers of Paris. At the same time Eugene de Beauharnais was Venerable of the
lodge of St. Eugene in Paris. Having come to Italy with the title of Viceroy, the Grand
Orient of Milan named him Master and Sovereign Commander of the Supreme
Council of the thirty-second grade, that is to say, accorded him the greatest honour
which could be given him according to the Statutes of the Order. Bernadotte was a
Mason. His son Oscar was Grand Master of the Swedish lodge. In the different lodges
of Paris were successively initiated, Alexander, Duke of Wurtemburg; the Prince Ber-
nard of Saxe-Weimar, even the Persian Ambassador, Askeri Khan. The President of
the Senate, Count de Lacipede, presided over the Grand Orient of France, which had
for officers of honour the Generals Kellerman, Messina, and Soult. Princes, Ministers,

the same time, closely, their own opportunities for the development of the deadly designs of the Sect. Then, they obtained the first places in his Empire for themselves. They put as much mischief into the measures of relief given to conscience as they could. They established a fatal supremacy for secularism in the matter of education. They brought dissension between the Pope and the Emperor. They caused the second confiscation of the States of the Church. They caused and continued to the end, the imprisonment of Pius VII. They were at the bottom of every attack made by Napoleon while Emperor upon the rights of the Church, the freedom and indepen-

Marshals, Officers, Magistrates, all the men, in fine, remarkable for their glory or considerable by their position, ambitioned to be made Masons. The women even wished to have their lodges into which entered Mesdames de Vaudemont, de Carignan, de Gerardin, de Narbonne and many other ladies."

Frère Clavel, in his picturesque history of Freemasonry, says that, "Of all these high personages the Prince Cambaceres was the one who most occupied himself with Masonry. He made it his duty to rally to Masonry all the men in France who were influential by their official position, by their talent, or by their fortune. The personal services which he rendered to many of the brethren, the eclat which he caused to be given to the lodges in bringing to their sittings by his example and invitations all those illustrious amongst the military and judicial professions and others, contributed powerfully to the fusion of parties and to the consolidation of the imperial throne. In effect under his brilliant and active administration the lodges multiplied ad infinitum. They were composed of the elect of French society. They became a point of re-union for the partisans of the existing and of passed regimes. They celebrated in them the feasts of the Emperor. They read in them the bulletins of his victories before they were made public by the press, and able men organized the enthusiasm which gradually took hold of all minds."

dence of the Supreme Pontiff, and the well-being of religion.

But the chief mistake of Napoleon was the encouragement he gave to Freemasonry. It served his purpose admirably for a while, that is so long as he served the present and ultimate views of the conspiracy; for a conspiracy Masonry ever was and ever will be. Even if Cambaceres, Talleyrand, Fouché, and the old leaders of the Illuminati, whom he had taken into his confidence and richly rewarded, should be satisfied, there was a mass of others whom no reward could conciliate, and who, filled with the spirit of the Sect, were sure to be ever on the look out for the means to advance the designs of Weishaupt and his inner circle. That inner circle never ceased its action. It held the members of the Sect, whom it not only permitted but assisted to attain high worldly honours, completely in its power, and hence in absolute subjection. For them as well as for the humblest member of the secret conclave, the poisoned aqua tophona and the dagger were ready to do the work of certain death should they lack obedience to those depraved fanatics of one diabolical idea, who were found worthy to be selected by their fellow conspirators to occupy the highest place of infamy and secret power. These latter scattered secretly amidst the rank and file of the lodges, hundreds of Argus-eyed, skilled plotters, who kept the real power of inner or high Masonry in the hands of its hidden masters. Masonry from this secret vantage ground ceaselessly conspired during the Empire. It assisted the conquest of the victor of Austerlitz and Jena; and if Deschamps, who quotes from the most reliable sources, is to be trusted, it actually did more for these victories than the great military leader himself. Through its instrumentality the resources of the enemies of Napoleon were never at hand, the designs of the Austrian and other generals opposed to him were thwarted, treason was rife in their camps, and information fatal to their designs was conveyed to the French commander. Masonry was then on his side, and as now the secret resources of the Order, its power of hidden influence and espionage were placed at the disposal of the cause it served. But when Masonry had reason to fear that Napoleon's power might be perpetuated; when his alliance with the Imperial Family of Austria, and above all, when the consequence of that alliance, an heir to his throne, caused danger to the universal republic it could otherwise assure itself of at his death; when, too, he began to show a coldness for the sect, and sought means to prevent it from the propagandism of its diabolical aims, then it became his enemy, and his end was not far off.[2] Distracting councils prevailed in his cabinet. His opponents began to get information regarding his movements, which he had obtained previously of theirs. Members of the sect urged on his mad expedition to Moscow, His resources were paralyzed; and he was, in one word, sold by secret, invisible foes into the hands of his enemies. In Germany, Weishaupt and his party, still living on in dark intrigue, prepared secretly for his downfall. His generals were beaten in

[2] Deschamps says that it was at this period that the order of the Templars (for Masonry is divided into any amount of rites which exercise one over the other a kind of influence in proportion to the members of the inner grades which they contain) was resuscitated in France. It publicly interred one of its members from the Church of St. Antoine. The funeral oration of Jacques Molay was publicly pronounced. Napoleon permitted this. The danger his permission created was foreseen, and M. de Maistre writes:—"A very remarkable phenomenon is that of the resuscitation of Freemasonry in France, so far, that a brother has been interred solemnly in Paris with all the attributes and ceremonies of the order. The Master who reigns in France does not leave it to be even suspected that such a thing can exist in France without his leave. Judging from his known character and from his ideas upon secret societies, how then can the thing be explained? Is he the Chief, or dupe, or perhaps the one and the other of a society which he thinks he knows, and which mocks him." Illustrating these remarks we have the comments of M. Bagot in his *Cades des Franc-Maçons*, p. 183:—"The Imperial Government took advantage of its omnipotence, to which so many men, so many institutions, yielded so complacently, in order to dominate over Masonry. The latter became neither afraid nor revolted. What did it desire in effect? To extend its empire—"It permitted itself to become subject to despotism in order to become sovereign." This gives us the whole reason why Masonry first permitted Napoleon to rule, then to reign, then to conquer, and finally to fall.

detail. He was betrayed, hoodwinked, and finally led to his deposition and ruin. He then received with a measure, pressed down and overflowing, and shaken together, the gratitude of the father of lies, incarnate in Freemasonry, in the Illuminati, and kindred Atheist secret societies. Banished to Elba he was permitted to return to France only in order to meet the fate of an outcast and a prisoner upon the rock of St. Helena, where he died abandoned and persecuted by the dark Sect which had used, abused, and betrayed him. So it has continued, as we shall see, to use, to abuse, and to betray every usurper or despot whom it lures into its toils.

XI

FREEMASONRY AFTER THE FALL OF NAPOLEON

THE many intrigues of that very same body of Illuminati who had planned and executed the Revolution, then created successively the Directory, the Consulate, and the Empire in France, as they now posed in a new capacity as friends to the return of Monarchy in Europe generally. This they did for the purposes of the Freemasons, and in order to keep the power they wielded so long in their own hands, and in the hands of their party. Now, I wish you to note, that Weishaupt, the father of the Illuminati, and the fanatical and deep director of all its operations, was even then living in power and security at Coburg-Gotha, and that his wily confederates were ministers in every court of Europe. Then, as now, the invincible determination with which they secreted their quality from the eyes of monarchs as well as of the general public, enabled them to pose in any character or capacity without fear of being detected as Freemasons, or at least as Illuminati. Since the reign of Frederick the Great, they filled the Court of Berlin. Many minor German Princes continued to be Freemasons. The Duke of Brunswick was the central figure in the first Masonic conspiracy, and though, with the hypocrisy co mm on to the Sect, he issued a declaration highly condemnatory of his fellows, it is generally believed that he remained to the end attached to the "regeneration of humanity" in the interests of Atheism. The Court of Vienna was more or less Masonic since the reign of the wretched Joseph II. Alexander of Russia was educated by La Harpe, a Freemason, and at the very period when called upon to play a principal part in the celebrated "Holy Alliance," he was under the hidden guidance of others of the Illuminati. Fessler, an apostate Austrian religious, the Councillor of Joseph II, after having abjured Christianity, remained, while professing a respect for religion, its most determined enemy. He founded what is known as the Tugendbund, a society by which German Freemasonry put on a certain Christian covering, in order more securely to outlive the reaction against Atheism, and to de-Christianize the world again at a better opportunity. The Tugendbund refused to receive Jews, and devised many other means to deceive Christians to become substantially Freemasons without incurring Church censures or going against ideas then adverse to the old Freemasonry, which, nevertheless, continued to exist as satanic as ever under Christian devices.

In France, the Illuminati of the schools of Wilhelmsbad and Lyons continued their machinations without much change of front, though they covered themselves with that impenetrable secrecy which the sect has found so convenient for disarming public suspicion while pursuing its aims. Possessing means of deceiving the outside world, and capable of using every kind of hypocrisy and ruse, the Freemasons of both France and Germany plotted at this period with more secure secrecy and success than ever. There is nothing which Freemasonry dreads more than light. It is the one thing it cannot stand. Therefore, it has always taken care to provide itself with adepts and allies able to disarm public suspicion in its regard. Should outsiders endeavour to find out its real character and aims, it takes refuge at once under the semblance of puerility, of harmless amusement, of beneficence, or even of half-witted simplicity. It is content to be laughed at, in order not to be found out. But it is for all its puerility the same dangerous foe to Christianity, law, legitimacy, and order, which it proved itself to be before and during the first French Revolution, and which it will continue to be until the world has universal reason to know

the depth, the malignity, and the extent of its remorseless designs.[1]

At the period of the reaction against Bonaparte
it seems to have taken long and wise counsel. When
Talleyrand found that Weishaupt and the inner Masonry no longer approved of Napoleon's autocracy,

[1] At the Council of Verona, held by the European sovereigns in 1822, to guard their
thrones and peoples from the revolutionary excesses which threatened Spain, Naples,
ana Piedmont, the Count Haugwitz, Minister of the King of Prussia, who then accompanied his master, made the following speech:—

"Arrived at the end of my career, I believe it to be my duty to cast a glance upon the
secret societies whose power menaces humanity to-day more than ever. Their history
is so bound up with that of my life that I cannot refrain from publishing it once more
and from giving some details regarding it.

"My natural disposition, and my education, having excited in me so great a desire
for information that I could not content myself with ordinary knowledge, I wished to
penetrate into the very essence of things. But shadow follows light, thus an insatiable
curiosity develops itself in proportion to the efforts which one makes to penetrate further into the sanctuary of science. These two sentiments impelled me to enter into the
society of Freemasons.

"It is well known that the first step which one makes in the order is little calculated to
satisfy the mind. That is precisely the danger to be dreaded for the inflammable imagination of youth. Scarcely had I attained my majority, when, not only did I find myself at
the head of Masonry, but what is more, I occupied a distinguished place in the chapter
of high grades. Before I had the power of knowing myself, before I could comprehend
the situation in which I had rashly engaged myself, I found myself charged with the superior direction of the Masonic reunions of a part of Prussia, of Poland, and of Russia.
Masonry was, at that time, divided into two parts, in its secret labour. The first place in
its emblems, the explanation of the philosopher's stone: Deism and non-Atheism was
the religion of these Sectaries. The central seat of their labours was at Berlin, under the
direction of the Doctor Zumdorf. It was not the same with the other part of which the

he managed very adroitly that the Emperor should grow cold with him. He was thus free to take adverse measures against his master, and to prepare himself for the coming change. The whole following of Bonaparte recruited from the Illuminati were ready to betray him. They could compass the fall of

Duke of Brunswick was the apparent chief. In open conflict between themselves, the two parties gave each other the hand in order to obtain the dominion of the world, to conquer thrones, to serve themselves with Kings as an order, such was their aim. It would be superfluous to explain to you in what manner, in my ardent curiosity, I came to know the secrets of the one party and of the other. The truth is, the secret of the two Sects is no longer a mystery for me. That secret is revolting.

"It was in the year 1777, that I became charged with the direction of one part of the Prussian lodges, three or four years before the Convent of Wilhelmsbad and the invasion of the lodges by Illuminism. My action extended even over the brothers dispersed throughout Poland and Russia. If I did not myself see it, I could not give myself even a plausible explanation of the carelessness with which Governments have been able to shut their eyes to such a disorder, a veritable state within a State. Not only were the chiefs in constant correspondence, and employed particular cyphers, but even they reciprocally sent emissaries one to another. To exercise a dominating influence over thrones, such was our aim, as it had been of the Knight Templars.

"'I thus acquired the firm conviction that the drama commenced in 1788 and 1789, the French Revolution, the regicide with all its horrors, not only was then resolved upon, but was even the result of these associations and oaths, &c.

"Of all my contemporaries of that epoch there is not one left. My first care was to communicate to William III all my discoveries. We came to the conclusion that all the Masonic associations, from the most humble even to the very highest degrees, could not do otherwise than employ religious sentiments in order to execute plans the most criminal, and make use of the first in order to cover the second. This conviction, which His Highness Prince William held in common with me, caused me to take the firm resolution of renouncing Masonry."

the tyrant, but the difficulty for them was to find one suitable to put in his place. It was decreed in their highest council that whosoever should come upon the throne of France, should be as far removed as possible from being a friend to Catholicism or to any principle sustaining true religion. They therefore determined that, if at all possible, no member of the ancient House should reign; and as soon as the allied sovereigns who were for the most part non-Catholic, had crushed Napoleon, these French Masons demanded the Protestant and Masonic King of Holland for King in France. This failing, they contrived by Masonic arts to obtain the first places in the Provisional Government which succeeded Napoleon. They endeavoured to make the most of the inevitable, and to rule the incoming Louis XVIII in the interests of their sect and to the detriment of the Church and of Christianity.

Notwithstanding the fact that they had shown open hostility to himself and to his house, Louis XVIII, strange to say, favoured the Illuminati. Talleyrand was made minister, and the other advanced Freemasons of the Empire—Sieyès, Cambacérès, Fouché, and the rest—obtained place and power. These men at once applied themselves to subvert the sentiment of reaction in favour of the monarchy and of religion. Soon, Louis XVIII gave the world the sad spectacle of a man prepared at their bidding to cut his own throat. He dissolved a Parliament of ultra loyalists because they were too loyal to him. The Freemasons took care that his next Parliament should be full of its own creatures. They also wrung from the King, under the plea of freedom of the press, permission to deluge the country anew with the infidel and immoral publications of Voltaire and his confederates, and with newspapers and periodicals, which proved disastrous to his house, to royalty, and to Christianity, in France. These led before long to the attempt upon the life of the Duke of Berry, to the revolution against Charles X, to the elevation of the son of the Grand Master, Égalité, as Constitutional King, and to all the revolutionary results that have since distracted and disgraced unfortunate France. But much as Freemasonry effected in that country, it was not there but in peaceful Italy that its illuminated machinations produced the worst and most wide-spread fruits of death.

XII

KINDRED SECRET SOCIETIES
IN EUROPE

WE HAVE seen that the use made of Freemasonry by the Atheists of the last century was a very elastic one. As it came from England it had all the qualities required by the remorseless revolutionists, who so eagerly and so ably employed it for their purposes. Its hypocritical professions of Theism, of acceptation of the Bible, and of beneficence; its terrible oaths of secrecy; its grotesque and absurd ceremonial, to which any meaning from the most silly to the deepest and darkest could be given; its ascending degrees, each one demanding additional secrets, to be kept not only from outsiders, but from the lower degrees; the death penalty for indiscretion or disobedience; the system of mystery capable of any extension; the hidden hierarchy; in a word, all its qualities could be improved and elaborated at will by the Infidels of the Continent who had made British Masonry their own. Soon the strict subjection of all subordinate lodges to whatever Grand Orient or Mother Lodge they spring from, and on which they depend, and, above all, the complete understanding between the directors of the Masonic "powers," that is of the different rites into which the Masonry is divided, placed its entire government in a select ruling body, directed in turn by a small committee of the ablest conspirators, elected by and known to that body alone. The whole rank and file of Masonry receive their orders at present from this inner body, who are unknown to the mere masons of the lodges. The members of the committee deputed by the lodges are able to testify to the fact of the authenticity of the orders. Those who rule from the hidden recesses take care that these deputies shall be men worthy of confidence. A lodge, therefore, has its masters, it officers, and management; but its orders come through a channel that appears to be nothing, whereas it is everything in the movement of the whole mass. Thus it happens that the master of a lodge or the grand master of a province, or of a nation, whose high-sounding titles may make him seem to outsiders to be everything, is in reality often nothing at all in the actual government of Masonry. The real power rests with the hidden committee of direction, and confidential agents, who move almost invisibly amongst the officers and members of the lodges. These hidden agents of iniquity are vigilant spies, secret "wire pullers," who are seldom promoted to any office, but content themselves with the real power which they are selected to use with dexterity and care.

It was through this system that Weishaupt obtained the adoption of illuminated Masonry at the convent of Wilhelmsbad. Through the machinations of Knigge he obtained from the delegates there assembled the approval of his plan that the ultimate end of Freemasonry and all secret plotting should be—1°, Pantheism—a form of Atheism which flatters Masonic pride. 2°, Communism of goods, women, and general concerns. 3°, That the means to arrive at these ends should be the destruction of the Church, and of all forms of Christianity; the obliteration of every kind of supernatural belief; and, finally, the removal of all existing human governments to make way for a universal republic in which the Utopian ideas of complete liberty from existing social, moral, and religious restraint, absolute equality, and social fraternity, should reign. When these ends should be attained, but not till then, the secret work of the Atheistic Freemasons should cease.

At the convent of Wilhelmsbad, Weishaupt had the means taken to carry out this determination. There Masonry became one organized Atheistic mass, while being still permitted to assume many fantastic shapes. The Knights Rosicrucian, the Templars, the Knights of Beneficence, the Brothers of Amity were strictly united to Illuminated Masonry. All could be reached through Masonry itself. All were placed under the same government. Masonry was made more elastic than ever. When, as in the cases of Ireland and Poland, an enslaved nationality should be found, which the supreme Invisible Directory wished to revolutionize, and when, at the same time, the existing respect for the words of the Vicar of Christ made Masonry hateful, a secret political society was ordered to be formed on the plan of Freemasonry, but with some other name. It too put on, after the example of Masonry itself, the semblance of zeal and respect for religion, but it was bound to have horrible oaths, ascending degrees, centres, the terrible death penalty for indiscretion or treason, to be, in essence, and in every sense, if not in name, a society identical with Freemasonry. The supreme direction of the Revolution was to contrive by sure means to have adepts high and powerful in its management; and the society was, even if founded to defend the Catholic religion, thus sure, sooner or later, to diverge from the Church and to become hostile to religion and to its ministers. The Atheistic revolutionists of the Continent in the last century learned to perfection the art to effect this; and hence the ready assistance which men who were murdering priests in Paris and throughout France and Italy, gave to the Catholics of Ireland in 1798. Was it to relieve the Catholics of Ireland from persecution, while they themselves were to a far more frightful extent oppressing the Catholic Church, the Catholic priesthood. Catholic religious, and Catholic people, for no other reason than the profession of the Catholic faith in France and Italy? By no means. They, at the very time, had already corrupted Irishmen. Some of these were open Infidels and others were Jacobite Freemasons of no particular attachment to any form of Christianity. They shared in Napoleon's indifference to religion, and were as ready to profess zeal for their Catholic fellow countrymen, as he and his soldiers were ready to profess "love" for the Alkoran and the Prophet in Egypt, or for St. Januarius in Naples. But they and their leaders in Black Masonry knew that once they could unite even the very best and truest Catholic men in Ireland into a secret society on such lines as I have described, they would soon find an entrance for Atheism into the country. They would not be wanting in means to win recruits by degrees from the best intentioned Catholics so bound by oaths, and so subjected to hidden influences. They were adepts at proselytism, especially amongst those who gave up liberty and will to unknown masters. But the agency of the Atheists of France was carried to work the mischief it intended for Ireland upon other Catholic lands. It forced its tyranny very soon upon Italy, Spain, Portugal, Switzerland, and the Rhenish provinces of Germany. That was bad enough, but it was not all. When the French revolutionary armies had departed from these countries, after the fall of Bonaparte, they left a deadly scourge that could not be removed behind them. That was the system of Atheistic organization of which we have been speaking, and which was not slow in producing its malignant fruits.

In Catholic Italy, where the scourge of the Revolution fell most heavily, the misfortune happened thus: The discontent consequent upon the multitude of political parties in that country gave the secret machinators of the Weishaupt school a splendid opportunity of again renewing their intrigues; while the miserable Government of the Bourbons in France, in permitting Freemasonry to flourish, afforded its supreme direction an opportunity to assist them in many ways. Public opinion in Germany was unripe for any Atheism unless veiled under the hypocritical pretences of the Tugendbund. In Italy, however, though religion was strong amongst all classes, the division of the country into small principalities caused the hopes of the revolutionists to be more sanguine than anywhere else, and the opportunity of dealing a blow at the temporal power of the Pope under the national pretext of a united Italy, was too great a temptation for the Supreme Masonic Directory to resist. Besides, it could not be forgotten by them, that in making past efforts the power of the Pope was the principal cause of their many failures. They rightly judged that the complete destruction of his temporal authority was essential to Atheism, and the first and most necessary step to their ultimate views upon all Christianity, and for the subjugation of the world to their sway. The temporal power was the stronghold, the rallying point of every legitimate authority in Europe. With a sure instinct of self-preservation, the Schismatical Lord of Russia, the Evangelical King of Prussia, the Protestant Governments of England, Denmark, and Sweden, as well as the ancient legitimate Catholic dynasties of Portugal, Austria, Bavaria, and Spain had determined at the Congress of Vienna on the restoration of the temporal dominions of the Pope. The Conservatives of Europe, whether Catholic, Protestant, or Schismatic, felt that while the States of the Church were preserved intact to the Head of the Catholic religion, their own rights would remain unquestioned—that to reach themselves his rights should be first assailed. The Atheistic conspiracy, guided now by old, experienced revolutionists, saw also that the conservatism of the world which they had to destroy in order to dominate in its stead, could not be undermined without first taking away the foundation of Christian civilization upon which it rested, and which unquestionably, even for Christian schismatics and heretics, was the temporal and the spiritual authority of the Pope. Having no idea of a divine preservation of the Christian religion, they judged that the destruction of the temporal power would lead inevitably to the destruction of the spiritual; and as experience proved that it would be useless to attempt to destroy both altogether, they then set all their agencies at work to destroy the temporal power first. They therefore determined to create and ferment to the utmost extent a political discontent amongst the populations of the different states into which the Italian Peninsula was divided. Now this was a difficult task in the face of the experience which the Italian people had gained of the revolutions and constant political changes brought by the French from the first attempt of the Republic to the last of the Empire. The Congress of Vienna restored most of the ancient Italian States as well as the States of the Church to the legitimate rulers. Peace and prosperity beyond what had been known for years began to reign in the Peninsula. The mass of the people were profoundly contented. They were more Catholic than ever, notwithstanding all that the revolutionary agents of France did to pervert them. But there remained a dangerous fraction amidst the population not at all satisfied with the change which had so much improved the nation generally. This fraction consisted of those individuals and their children who benefited by the revolutionary regime. They were the men who made themselves deputies in Rome, Naples, and elsewhere, and by the aid of French revolutionary bayonets seized upon Church property and became enriched by public spoliation. These still remained revolutionary to the core. Then, there was the interest effected by their party. And finally, there was that uneasy class, educated by the many cheap universities of the country in too great number, the sons of advocates and other profession- al men, who, tinged with liberalism, easily became the prey of the designing men who still remained addicted to the principles and were leagued in the secret organizations of Weishaupt and his fellow Atheists. Even one of these youths corrupted and excited to ambition by the adroit manipulation of these emissaries of Satan, still active, though more imperceptible than ever, would be sufficient to kin- dle a flame amongst his fellows capable of creating a wide discontent. Aided then by such elements, already at hand for their purposes, Weishaupt and his hidden Directory determined to kindle such a flame of Revolution in Italy as, in its effects, should, before long, do more harm to religion and order than even the French Revolution had caused in its sanguinary but brief career. They effected this by the formation, on the darkest lines of "illuminated" Masonry, of the terrible Sect of the Carbonari.

XIII

THE CARBONARI

IN this sect, the whole of the hitherto recognized principles of organized Atheism were perfected and intensified. In it, from the commencement, a cunning hypocrisy was the means most used as the best calculated to lead away a people Catholic to the very core. The first of the Carbonari of which we have any distinct notice appeared at a season when Atheism, directed by Weishaupt, was busy in forming everywhere secret associations for apparently no purpose other than political amelioration. He determined to try upon the peasantry of Italy the same arts which the French had intended for the Catholic peasantry of Ireland. The United Irishmen were banded together to demand amongst other things, Catholic Emancipation. Never had a people greater reason to rise against oppression than the Catholics of Ireland of that period. They were urged on to do so, however, by leaders who, in many instances, were not Catholic, and who had no political grievance, and whose aim was the formation in Ireland of an independent republic ruled, of course, by themselves, on the model of the one which was established then in France. That seemed to the Catholic the only way to get out of the heretical domination which had for such a lengthened period oppressed his country. Now, the Carbonari of Italy were at first formed for a purpose identical with that of the United Irishmen. They conspired to bring back their national independence ruined by the French, the freedom of their religion, and their rightful Bourbon sovereign. With them it was made an indispensable obligation that each member should be not only a Catholic, but a Catholic going regularly to the Sacraments. They took for their Grand Master, Jesus Christ our Lord. But, as I have said before, it is impossible for a secret society having a death penalty for breach of secret, having ascending degrees, and bound to blind obedience to hidden masters, to remain any appreciable length of time without falling under the domination of the Supreme Directory of organized Atheism. It was so with Carbonarism, which, having started on the purest Catholic and loyal lines, soon ended in being the very worst kind of secret society which Infidelity had then formed on the lines of Masonry. Very soon, Italian adepts in black Masonry invaded its ranks, the loudest in the protestation of religion and loyalty. Equally soon, these skilled, experienced, and unscrupulous veterans in dark intrigue obtained the mastery in its supreme direction, won over proselytes from fit conspirators, and had the whole association in their power. It was then easy to find abundant pretexts to excite the passions of the rank and file, to kindle hopes from revolution, to create political dissatisfaction, and to make the whole body of the Sect what it has actually become. Italian genius soon outstripped the Germans in astuteness; and as soon, perhaps sooner, than Weishaupt passed away, the supreme government of all the secret societies of the world was exercised by the Alta Vendita or highest lodge of the Italian Carbonari. The Alta Vendita ruled the blackest Freemasonry of France, Germany, and England; and until Mazzini wrenched the sceptre of the dark Empire from that body, it continued with consummate ability to direct the revolutions of Europe. It considered, with that wisdom peculiar to the children of darkness, that the conspiracy against the Holy See was the conspiracy in permanence. It employed its principal intrigues against the State, the surroundings, and the very person of the Pontiff. It had hopes, by its manipulations, to gain eventually, even the Pope himself, to betray the Christian cause, and then it well knew the universe would be placed at its feet. It left unmeasured freedom to the lodges of Masonry to carry on those revolutions of a political kind, which worked out the problems of the sect upon France, Spain, Italy, and other countries. It kept still greater movements to itself. The permanent instruction of this body to its adepts will give you an idea of its power, its policy, and its principles.

XIV

PERMANENT INSTRUCTION
OF THE ALTA VENDITA

"EVER since we have established ourselves as a body of action, and that order has commenced to reign in the bosom of the most distant lodge, as in that one nearest the centre of action, there is one thought which has profoundly occupied the men who aspire to universal regeneration. That is the thought of the enfranchisement of Italy, from which must one day come the enfranchisement of the entire world, the fraternal republic, and the harmony of humanity. That thought has not yet been seized upon by our brethren beyond the Alps. They believe that revolutionary Italy can only conspire in the shade, deal some strokes of the poniard to sbirri and traitors, and tranquilly undergo the yoke of events which take place beyond the Alps for Italy, but without Italy. This error has been fatal to us on many occasions. It is not necessary to combat it with phrases which would be only to propagate it. It is necessary to kill it by facts. Thus, amidst the cares which have the privilege of agitating the minds of the most vigorous of our lodges, there is one which we ought never to forget.

"The Papacy has at all times exercised a decisive action upon the affairs of Italy. By the hands, by the voices, by the pens, by the hearts of its innumerable bishops, priests, monks, nuns and people in all latitudes, the Papacy finds devotedness without end ready for martyrdom, and that to enthusiasm. Everywhere, whenever it pleases to call upon them, it has friends ready to die or lose all for its cause. This is an immense leverage which the Popes alone have been able to appreciate to its full power, and as yet they have used it only to a certain extent. To-day there is no question of reconstituting for ourselves that power, the prestige of which is for the moment weakened. Our final end is that of Voltaire and of the French Revolution, the destruction for ever of Catholicism and even of the Christian idea which, if left standing on the ruins of Rome, would be the resuscitation of Christianity later on. But to attain more certainly that result, and not prepare ourselves with gaiety of heart for reverses which adjourn indefinitely, or compromise for ages, the success of a good cause, we must not pay attention to those braggarts of Frenchmen, those cloudy Germans, those melancholy Englishmen, all of whom imagine they can kill Catholicism, now with an impure song, then with an illogical deduction; at another time, with a sarcasm smuggled in like the cottons of Great Britain. Catholicism has a life much more tenacious than that. It has seen the most implacable, the most terrible adversaries, and it has often had the malignant pleasure of throwing holy water on the tombs of the most enraged. Let us permit, then, our brethren of these countries to give themselves up to the sterile intemperance of their anti-Catholic zeal. Let them even mock at our Madonnas and our apparent devotion. With this passport we can conspire at our ease, and arrive little by little at the end we have in view.

"Now the Papacy has been for seventeen centuries inherent to the history of Italy. Italy cannot breathe or move without the permission of the Supreme Pastor. With him she has the hundred arms of Briareus, without him she is condemned to a pitiable impotence. She has nothing but divisions to foment, hatreds to break out, and hostilities to manifest themselves from the highest chain of the Alps to the lowest of the Appenines. We cannot desire such a state of things. It is necessary, then, to seek a remedy for that situation. The remedy is found. The Pope, whoever he may be, will never come to the secret societies. It is for the secret societies to come first to the Church, in the resolve to conquer the two.

"The work which we have undertaken is not the work of a day, nor of a month, nor of a year. It may last many years, a century perhaps, but in our ranks the soldier dies and the fight continues.

"We do not mean to win the Popes to our cause, to make them neophytes of our principles, and propagators of our ideas. That would be a ridiculous dream, no matter in what manner events may turn. Should cardinals or prelates, for example, enter, willingly or by surprise, in some manner, into a part of our secrets, it would be by no means a motive to desire their elevation to the See of Peter. That elevation would destroy us. Ambition alone would bring them to apostasy from us. The needs of power would force them to immolate us. That which we ought to demand, that which we should seek and expect, as the Jews expected the Messiah, is a Pope according to our wants. Alexander VI, with all his private crimes, would not suit us, for he never erred in religious matters. Clement XIV, on the contrary, would suit us from head to foot. Borgia was a libertine, a true sensualist of the eighteenth century strayed into the fifteenth. He has been anathematized, notwithstanding his vices, by all the voices of philosophy and incredulity, and he owes that anathema to the

vigour with which he defended the Church. Ganganelli gave himself over, bound hand and foot, to
the ministers of the Bourbons, who made him afraid,
and to the incredulous who celebrated his tolerance
and Ganganelli is become a very great Pope. He is
almost in the same condition that it is necessary for
us to find another, if that be yet possible. With that
we should march more surely to the attack upon the
Church than with the pamphlets of our brethren in
France, or even with the gold of England. Do you
wish to know the reason? It is because by that we
should have no more need of the vinegar of Han-
nibal, no more need of the powder of cannon, no
more need even of our arms. We have the little finger of the successor of St. Peter engaged in the plot,
and that little finger is of more value for our crusade
than all the Innocents, the Urbans, and the St. Ber-
nards of Christianity.

"We do not doubt that we shall arrive at that supreme term of all our efforts; but when? but how?
The unknown does not yet manifest itself. Nevertheless, as nothing should separate us from the plan
traced out; as, on the contrary, all things should tend
to it—as if success were to crown the work scarcely
sketched out to-morrow—we wish in this instruction which must rest a secret for the simple initiated,
to give to those of the Supreme Lodge, councils with

which they should enlighten the universality of the brethren, under the form of an instruction or memorandum. It is of special importance, and because of a discretion, the motives of which are transparent, never to permit it to be felt that these counsels are orders emanating from the Alta Vendita. The clergy is put too much in peril by it, that one can at the present hour permit oneself to play with it, as with one of these small affairs or of these little princes upon which one need but blow to cause them to disappear.

"Little can be done with those old cardinals or with those prelates, whose character is very decided. It is necessary to leave them as we find them, incorrigible, in the school of Consalvi, and draw from our magazines of popularity or unpopularity the arms which will render useful or ridiculous the power in their hands. A word which one can ably invent and which one has the art to spread amongst certain honourable chosen families by whose means it descends into the cafes and from the cafes into the streets; a word can sometimes kill a man. If a prelate comes to Rome to exercise some public function from the depths of the provinces, know presently his character, his antecedents, his qualities, his defects above all things. If he is in advance, a declared enemy, an Albani, a Pallotta, a Bemetti, a Delia Genga, a Riverola, envelope him in all the snares which you can place beneath his feet; create for him one of those reputations which will frighten little children and old women; paint him cruel and sanguinary; recount, regarding him, some traits of cruelty which can be easily engraved in the minds of people. When foreign journals shall gather for us these recitals, which they will embellish in their turn (inevitably because of their respect for truth), show, or rather cause to be shown, by some respectable fool those papers where the names and the excesses of the personages implicated are related. As France and England, so Italy will never be wanting in facile pens which know how to employ themselves in these lies so useful to the good cause. With a newspaper, the language of which they do not understand, but in which they will see the name of their delegate or judge, the people have no need of other proofs. They are in the infancy of liberalism; they believe in liberals, as, later on, they will believe in us, not knowing very well why.

"Crush the enemy whoever he may be; crush the powerful by means of lies and calumnies; but especially crush him in the egg. It is to the youth we must go. It is that which we must seduce; it is that which we must bring under the banner of the secret societies. In order to advance by steps, calculated but sure, in that perilous way, two things are of the first necessity. You ought to have the air of being simple as doves, but you must be prudent as the serpent. Your fathers, your children, your wives themselves, ought always to be ignorant of the secret which you carry in your bosoms. If it pleases you, in order the better to deceive the inquisitorial eye, to go often to confession, you are as by right authorised to preserve the most absolute silence regarding these things. You know that the least revelation, that the slightest indication escaped from you in the tribunal of penance, or elsewhere, can bring on great calamities and that the sentence of death is already pronounced upon the revealer, whether voluntary or involuntary.

"Now then, in order to secure to us a Pope in the manner required, it is necessary to fashion for that Pope a generation worthy of the reign of which we dream. Leave on one side old age and middle life, go to the youth, and, if possible, even to infancy. Never speak in their presence a word of impiety or impurity. *Maxima debetur puero reverentia.* Never forget these words of the poet for they will preserve you from licences which it is absolutely essential to guard against for the good of the cause. In order to reap profit at the home of each family, in order to give yourself the right of asylum at the domestic hearth, you ought to present yourself with all the appearance of a man grave and moral. Once your reputation is established in the colleges, in the gymnasiums, in the universities, and in the seminaries—once that you shall have captivated the confidence of professors and students, so act that those who are principally engaged in the ecclesiastical state should love to seek your conversation. Nourish their souls with the splendours of ancient Papal Rome. There is always at the bottom of the Italian heart a regret for Republican Rome. Excite, enkindle those natures so full of warmth and of patriotic fire. Offer them at first, but always in secret, inoffensive books, poetry resplendent with national emphasis; then little by little you will bring your disciples to the degree of cooking desired. When upon all the points of the ecclesiastical state at once, this daily work shall have spread our ideas as the light, then you will be able to appreciate the wisdom of the counsel in which we take the initiative.

"Events, which in our opinion, precipitate themselves too rapidly, go necessarily in a few months' time to bring on an intervention of Austria. There are fools who in the lightness of their hearts please themselves in casting others into the midst of perils, and, meanwhile, there are fools who at a given hour drag on even wise men. The revolution which they meditate in Italy will only end in misfortunes and persecutions. Nothing is ripe, neither the men nor the things, and nothing shall be for a long time yet; but from these evils you can easily draw one new chord, and cause it to vibrate in the hearts of the young clergy. That is the hatred of the stranger. Cause the German to become ridiculous and odious even before his foreseen entry. With the idea of the Pontifical supremacy, mix always the old memories of the wars of the priesthood and the Empire. Awaken the smouldering passions of the Guelphs and the Ghibellines, and thus you will obtain for yourselves the reputation of good Catholics and pure patriots.

"That reputation will open the way for our doctrines to pass to the bosoms of the young clergy, and go even to the depths of convents. In a few years the young clergy will have, by the force of events, invaded all the functions. They will govern, administer, and judge. They will form the council of the Sovereign. They will be called upon to choose the Pontiff who will reign; and that Pontiff, like the greater part of his contemporaries, will be necessarily imbued with the Italian and humanitarian principles which we are about to put in circulation. It is a little grain of mustard which we place in the earth, but the sun of justice will develop it even to be a great power, and you will see one day what a rich harvest that little seed will produce.

"In the way which we trace for our brethren there are found great obstacles to conquer, difficulties of more than one kind to surmount. They will be overcome by experience and by perspicacity; but the end is beautiful. What does it matter to put all the sails to the wind in order to attain it. You wish to revolutionize Italy? Seek out the Pope of whom we give the portrait. You wish to establish the reign of the elect upon the throne of the prostitute of Babylon? Let the clergy march under your banner in the belief always that they march under the banner of the Apostolic Keys. You wish to cause the last vestige of tyranny and of oppression to disappear? Lay your nets like Simon Barjona. Lay them in the depths of sacristies, seminaries, and convents, rather than in the depths of the sea, and if you will precipitate nothing you will give yourself a draught of fishes more miraculous than his. The fisher of fishes will become a fisher of men. You will bring yourselves as friends around the Apostolic Chair. You will have fished up a Revolution in Tiara and Cope, marching with Cross and banner—a Revolution which needs only to be spurred on a little to put the four quarters of the world on fire.

"Let each act of your life tend then to discover the Philosopher's Stone. The alchemists of the middle ages lost their time and the gold of their dupes in the quest of this dream. That of the secret societies will be accomplished for the most simple of reasons, because it is based on the passions of man. Let us not be discouraged then by a check, a reverse, or a defeat. Let us prepare our arms in the silence of the lodges, dress our batteries, flatter all passions the most evil and the most generous, and all lead us to think that our plans will succeed one day above even our most improbable calculations."

This document reveals the whole line of action followed since by the Italian Revolutionists. It gives also a fair insight into tactics with which other European countries have been made familiar by Freemasonry generally. But we are in possession of what appears to me a still more striking document, written for the benefit of the Piedmontese lodges of the Carbonari, by one of the Alta Vendita, whose pseudonym was Piccolo Tigre—Little Tiger. I may here mention that the custom of taking these fanciful appelations has been common to the secret societies from the very beginning. Arouet became Voltaire, the notorious Baron Knigge was called Philo, Baron Dittfort was called Minos, a custom adopted by the principal chiefs of the dark Atheistic conspiracy then and since. The first leader or grand chief of the Alta Vendita was a corrupt Italian nobleman who took the name of Nubius. From such documents as he, before his death, managed, in revenge for being sacrificed by the party of Mazzini, as we shall see, to have communicated to the authorities of Rome; or which were found by the vigilance of the Roman detective police; we find that his funds, and the funds for carrying on the deep and dark conspiracy in which he and his confederates were engaged, came chiefly from rich German Jews. Jews, in fact, from the commencement, played always a prominent part in the conspiracies of Atheism. They do so still. Piccolo Tigre, who seems to have been the most active agent of Nubius, was a Jew. He travelled under the appearance of an itinerant banker and jeweller. This character of moneylender or usurer disarmed suspicion regarding himself and such of his confederates as he had occasion to call upon in his peregrinations. Of course he had the protection of the Masonic body everywhere. The most desperate revolutionists were generally the most desperate scoundrels otherwise. They were gamblers, spendthrifts, and the very class with which an usurious Jew would be expected to have money dealings. Piccolo Tigre thus travelled safely; and brought safely to the superior lodges of the Carbonari, such instructions as the Alta Vendita thought proper to give. In the document referred to, which I shall now read for you, it will be seen how anxious the Secret Directory were to make use of the common form of Masonry notwithstanding the contempt they had for the bons vivants who only learned from the craft how to become drunkards and liberals. Beyond the Masons, and unknown to them, though formed generally from them, lay the deadly secret conclave which, nevertheless, used and directed them for the ruin of the world and of their own selves. The next chapter contains a translation of the document, or "instructions," as it was called, addressed by Piccolo Tigre to the Piedmontese lodges of the Carbonari.

XV

LETTER OF PICCOLO TIGRE

"IN the impossibility in which our brothers and friends find themselves, to say, as yet, their last word, it has been judged good and useful to propagate the light everywhere, and to set in motion all that which aspires to move. For this reason we do not cease to recommend to you, to affiliate persons of every class to every manner of association, no matter of what kind, only provided that mystery and secrecy should be the dominant characteristics. All Italy is covered with religious confraternities, and with penitents of divers colours. Do not fear to slip in some of your people into the very midst of these flocks, led as they are by a stupid devotion. Let our agents study with care the personnel of these confraternity men, and they will see that little by little, they will not be wanting in a harvest. Under a pretext the most futile, but never political or religious, create by yourselves, or, better yet, cause to be created by others, associations, having commerce, industry, music, the fine arts, etc., for object.[1] Reunite in one place or another—in the sacristies or chapels even—these tribes of yours as yet ignorant: put them under the pastoral staff of some virtuous priest, well known, but credulous and easy to be deceived. Then infiltrate the poison into those chosen hearts; infiltrate it in little doses, and, as if by chance. Afterwards, upon reflection, you will yourselves be astonished at your success.

"The essential thing is to isolate a man from his family, to cause him to lose his morals. He is sufficiently disposed by the bent of his character to flee from household cares, and to run after easy pleasures and forbidden joys. He loves the long conversations of the cafe and the idleness of shows. Lead

[1] Mazzini, after exhorting his followers to attract as many of the higher classes as possible to the secret plotting, which has resulted in united Italy, and is meant to result in republican Italy as a prelude to republican Europe, says "Associate, associate. All is contained in that word. The secret societies can give an irresistible force to the party who are able to invoke them. Do not fear to see them divided. The more they are divided the better it will be. All of them advance to the same end by different paths. The secret will be often unveiled. So much the better. The secret is necessary to give security to members, but a certain transparency is necessary to strike fear into those wishing to remain stationary. When a great number of associates who receive the word of command to scatter an idea abroad and make it public opinion, can concert even for a moment they will find the old edifice pierced in all its parts, and falling, as if by a miracle, at the least breath of progress. They will themselves be astonished to see kings, lords, men of capital, priests, and all those who form the carcass of the old social edifice, fly before the sole power of public opinion. Courage, then, and perseverance."

him along, sustain him, give him an importance of some kind or other; discreetly teach him to grow weary of his daily labours, and by this management, after having separated him from his wife and from his children, and after having shown him how painful are all his duties, you will then excite in him the desire of another existence. Man is a born rebel. Stir up the desire of rebellion until it becomes a conflagration, but in such a manner that the conflagration may not break out. This is a preparation for the grand work that you should commence. When you shall have insinuated into a few souls disgust for family and for religion (the one nearly always follows in the wake of the other), let fall some words which will provoke the desire of being affiliated to the nearest lodge. That vanity of the citizen or the burgess, to belong to Freemasonry, is something so common and so universal that it always makes me wonder at human stupidity. I begin to be astonished at not seeing the entire world knock at the gates of all the Venerables, and demand from these gentlemen the honour to be one of the workmen chosen for the reconstruction of the temple of Solomon. The prestige of the unknown exercises upon men a certain kind of power, that they prepare themselves with trembling for the phantasmagoric trials of the initiation and of the fraternal banquet.

"To find oneself a member of a lodge, to feel oneself called upon to guard from wife and children, a secret which is never confided to you, is for certain natures a pleasure and an ambition. The lodges, to-day, can well create gourmands, they will never bring forth citizens. There is too much dining amongst right worshipful and right reverend brethren of all the Ancients. But they form a place of depot, a kind of stud (breeding ground), a centre through which it is necessary to pass before coming to us. The lodges form but a relative evil, an evil tempered by a false philanthropy, and by songs yet more false as in France. All that is too pastoral and too gastronomic; but it is an object which it is necessary to encourage without ceasing. In teaching a man to raise his glass to his lips you become possessed of his intelligence and of his liberty, you dispose of him, turn him round about, and study him. You divine his inclinations, his affections, and his tendencies; then, when he is ripe for us, we direct him to the secret society of which Freemasonry can be no more than the antechamber.

"The Alta Vendita desires that under one pretence or another, as many princes and wealthy persons as possible should be introduced into the Masonic lodges. Princes of a sovereign house, and those who have not the legitimate hope of being kings by the grace of God, all wish to be kings by the grace of a Revolution. The Duke of Orleans is a Freemason, the Prince of Carignan was one also. There are not wanting in Italy and elsewhere, those amongst them, who aspire to the modest-enough honours of the symbolic apron and trowel. Others of them are disinherited and proscribed. Flatter all of their number who are ambitious of popularity; monopolize them for Freemasonry. The Alta Vendita will afterwards see what it can do to utilize them in the cause of progress. A prince who has not a kingdom to expect, is a good fortune for us. There are many of them in that plight. Make Freemasons of them. The lodge will conduct them to Carbonarism. A day will come, perhaps, when the Alta Vendita will deign to affiliate them. While awaiting they will serve as birdlime for the imbeciles, the intriguing, the bourgeoisie, and the needy. These poor princes will serve our ends, while thinking to labour only for their own. They form a magnificent sign board, and there are always fools enough to be found who are ready to compromise themselves in the service of a conspiracy, of which some prince or other seems to be the ringleader.

"Once that a man, that a prince, that a prince especially, shall have commenced to grow corrupt, be persuaded that he will hardly rest upon the declivity.

There is little morality even amongst the most moral of the world, and one goes fast in the way of that progress. Do not then be dismayed to see the lodges flourish, while Carbonarism recruits itself with difficulty. It is upon the lodges that we count to double our ranks. They form, without knowing it, our preparatory novitiate. They discourse without end upon the dangers of fanaticism, upon the happiness of social equality, and upon the grand principles of religious liberty. They launch amidst their feastings thundering anathemas against intolerance and persecution. This is positively more than we require to make adepts. A man imbued with these fine things is not very far from us. There is nothing more required than to enlist him. The law of social progress is there, and all there. You need not take the trouble to seek it elsewhere. In the present circumstances never lift the mask. Content yourselves to prowl about the Catholic sheepfold, but as good wolves seize in the passage the first lamb who offers himself in the desired conditions. The burgess has much of that which is good for us, the prince still more. For all that, these lambs must not be permitted to turn themselves into foxes like the infamous Carignan. The betrayal of the oath is a sentence of death; and all those princes whether they are weak or cowardly, ambitious or repentant, betray us, or denounce us. As good fortune would have it, they know little, in fact not anything, and they cannot come upon the trace of our true mysteries. "Upon the occasion of my last journey to France, I saw with profound satisfaction that our young initiated exhibited an extreme ardour for the diffusion of Carbonarism; but I also found that they rather precipitated the movement a little. As I think, they converted their religious hatred too much into a political hatred. The conspiracy against the Roman See should not confound itself with other projects. We are exposed to see germinate in the bosom of secret societies, ardent ambitions; and the ambitious, once masters of power, may abandon us. The route which we follow is not as yet sufficiently well traced so as to deliver us up to intriguers and tribunes. It is of absolute necessity to de-Catholicise the world. And an ambitious man, having arrived at his end, will guard himself well from seconding us. The Revolution in the Church is the Revolution *en permanence*. It is the necessary overthrowing of thrones and dynasties. Now an ambitious man cannot really wish these things. We see higher and farther. Endeavour, therefore, to act for us, and to strengthen us. Let us not conspire except against Rome. For that, let us serve ourselves with all kinds of incidents; let us put to profit every kind of eventuality. Let us be principally on our guard against the exaggerations of zeal.

A good hatred, thoroughly cold, thoroughly calculated, thoroughly profound, is of more worth than all these artificial fires and all these declamations of the platform. At Paris they cannot comprehend this, but in London I have seen men who seized better upon our plan, and who associated themselves to us with more fruit. Considerable offers have been made to me. Presently we shall have a printing establishment at Malta placed at our disposal. We shall then be able with impunity, with a sure stroke, and under the British flag, to scatter from one end of Italy to the other, books, pamphlets, etc., which the Alta Vendita shall judge proper to put in circulation."

This document was issued in 1822. Since then, the instructions it gives have been constantly acted upon in the lodges of Carbonarism, not only in Italy but everywhere else. "Prowl about the Catholic sheepfold and seize the first lamb that presents himself in the required conditions." This, and the order to get into Catholic confraternities, were as well executed by the infamous Carey under the influence of "No. 1," as they were by any Italian conspirator and assassin, under the personal inspiration of Piccolo Tigre. Carey, the loud-spoken Catholic—the Catholic who had Freemason or Orange friends able to assist him in the truly Masonic way of getting members of the craft as Town-Councillors, or Aldermen, or Members of Parliament—was, we now know, a true secret-society hypocrite of the genuine Italian type. He prowled with effect round the Catholic sheep-fold. He joined "with fruit" the confraternities of the Church.

Another curious instruction given by the Alta Vendita to the Carbonari of the lower lodges, is the way to catch a priest and make the good, simple man, unconsciously aid the designs of the revolutionary sectaries. In the permanent instruction of the Alta Vendita, given to all the lodges, you will recollect the passage I read for you relative to the giving of bad names to faithful Prelates who may be too knowing or too good to do the work of the Carbonari against conscience, God, and the souls of men, "Ably find out the words and the ways to make them unpopular" is the sum of that advice. Has it not been attempted amongst ourselves? But the main advice of the permanent instruction is to seduce the clergy. The ecclesiastic to be deceived is to be led on by patriotic ardour. He is to be blinded by a constant, though, of course, false, and fatal popularity. He is to be made believe that his course, so very pleasant to flesh and blood, is not only the most patriotic but the best for religion. "A free Church in a free State," was the cry with which the sectaries pulled down the altars, banished the religious, seized upon Church property, robbed the Pope, and despoiled the Propaganda. There were ecclesiastics so far deceived, at one time, as to be led away by these cries in Italy, and ecclesiastics have been deceived, if not by these, at least by cries as false and fatal elsewhere to our knowledge. The seduction of foremost ecclesiastics, prelates, and bishops, was the general policy of the sect at all times, and it remains so everywhere to this day.

The rank and file of the Carbonari had to do with local priests and local men of influence. These were, if possible, to be corrupted, unnerved, and seduced. Each Carbonaro was ordered to try and corrupt a fellow Christian, a man of family, by means that the devil himself incarnate could not devise better for the purpose.

At the end of his letter, Piccolo Tigre glances at means of corruption which he hoped then—and his hopes were soon realized to the full—to have in operation for the scattering of Masonic "light" throughout Italy. We have another document which will enable us to judge of the nature of this "light." It is contained in a letter from Vindex to Nubius, and was meant to cause the ideas of the Alta Vendita to pass through the lodges. It is found in that convenient form of questioning which the Sultan propounds to the Sheik-ul-Islam when he wants to make war. He puts his reasons in a set of questions, and the Sheik replies in as many answers. Then the war is right in the sight of Allah, and so all Islam go to fight in a war so sanctified. The new Islam does the same. A skilfully devised set of questions are posed for the consideration of one member of the Alta Vendita by another, and the answer which has been well concocted in secret conclave, is of course either given or implied to be given by the nature of the case. The horrible quality of the diabolical measures proposed by Vindex to Nubius in this form for the desired destruction of the Church, cannot be surpassed. If he discountenances assassination, it is not from fear or loathing of that frightful crime, but simply because it is not the best policy. He certainly did fall in upon the only blow that could—if that were possible, which, thank God, it is not—destroy the Church of God, and place, as he well says, Catholicism in the tomb. This is a translation of the document:—

CASTELLAMARE, 9th August, 1838.

"The murders of which our people render themselves culpable now in France, now in Switzerland, and always in Italy, are for us a shame and a remorse. It is the cradle of the world, illustrated by the epilogue of Cain and Abel, and we are too far in progress to content ourselves with such means. To what purpose does it serve to kill a man? To strike fear into the timid and to keep audacious hearts far from us? Our predecessors in Carbonarism did not understand their power. It is not in the blood of an isolated man, or even of a traitor, that it is necessary to exercise it; it is upon the masses. Let us not individualize crime. In order to grow great, even to the proportions of patriotism and of hatred for the Church, it is necessary to generalize it. A stroke of the dagger signifies nothing, produces nothing. What does the world care for a few unknown corpses cast upon the highway by the vengeance of secret societies? What matters it to the world, if the blood of a workman, of an artist, of a gentleman, or even of a prince, has flown in virtue of a sentence of Mazzini, or certain of his cut-throats playing seriously at the Holy Vehme? The world has not time to lend an ear to the last cries of the victim. It passes on and forgets: it is we, my Nubius, we alone, that can suspend its march. Catholicism has no more fear of a well-sharpened stiletto than monarchies have, but these two bases of social order can fall by corruption. Let us then never cease to corrupt. Tertullian was right in saying, that the blood of martyrs was the seed of Christians. Let us, then, not make martyrs, but let us popularise vice amongst the multitudes. Let us cause them to draw it in by their five senses;

to drink it in; to be saturated with it; and that land which Aretinus has sown is always disposed to receive lewd teachings. Make vicious hearts, and you will have no more Catholics. Keep the priest away from labour, from the altar, from virtue. Seek adroitly to otherwise occupy his thoughts and his hours. Make him lazy, a gourmand, and a patriot. He will become ambitious, intriguing, and perverse. You will thus have a thousand times better accomplished your task, than if you had blunted the point of your stiletto upon the bones of some poor wretches. I do not wish, nor do you any more, my friend Nubius, to devote my life to conspiracies, in order to be dragged along in the old ruts.

"It is corruption en masse that we have undertaken: the corruption of the people by the clergy, and the corruption of the clergy by ourselves; the corruption which ought, one day to enable us to put the Church in her tomb. I have recently heard one of our friends, laughing in a philosophic manner at our projects, say to us: 'in order to destroy Catholicism it is necessary to commence by suppressing woman.' The words are true in a sense; but since we cannot suppress woman, let us corrupt her with the Church, corruptio optimi pessima. The object we have in view is sufficiently good to tempt men such as we are; let us not separate ourselves from it for some miserable personal satisfaction of vengeance. The best poniard with which to strike the Church is corruption. To work, then, even to the very end."

The horrible programme of impurity here proposed was at once adopted. It was after all but an attempt more determined than ever, to spread the immorality of which Voltaire and his school were the apostles. At the time the Alta Vendita propounded this infernal plan they were resisting an inroad upon their authority on the part of Joseph Mazzini, just then coming into notoriety, who, however, overcame them.

Mazzini developed and taught, in his grandiloquent style, as well as practised the doctrine of assassination[2] which formed, we know, a part of the system of all secret societies, and which the Alta Vendita deprecated because they feared that it was

[2] The following extracts from the rules of the Carbonari of Italy, "Young Italy," will give an idea of the spirit and intent of the order as improved by the warlike and organizing genius of Mazzini:—

ART. I.—The society is formed for the indispensable destruction of all the Governments of the Peninsula and to form of Italy one sole State under a Republican Government.

ART. II.—Having experienced the horrible evils of absolute power and those yet greater of constitutional monarchies, we ought to work to found a Republic one and indivisible.

ART. XXX.—Those who do not obey the orders of the secret society, or who shall reveal its mysteries, shall be poniarded without remission. The same chastisement for traitors.

about to be employed, just then, against the members of their own body. Mazzini speaks of having arisen from his bed one morning fully satisfied as to the lawfulness of removing whomsoever he might be pleased to consider an enemy by the dagger, and fully determined to put that horrible principle into execution. He cherished it as the simplest means given to an oppressed people to free themselves from

ART. XXXI.—The secret tribunal shall pronounce the sentence and shall design one or two affiliated members for its immediate execution.

ART. XXXII.—Whoever shall refuse to execute the sentence shall be considered a perjurer, and as such shall be killed on the spot.

ART. XXXIII.—If the culpable individual escape he shall be pursued without intermission in every place, and he ought to be struck by an invisible hand, even should he take refuge in the bosom of his mother or in the tabernacles of Christ.

ART. XXXIV.—Every secret tribunal shall be competent not only to judge the culpable adepts, but also to cause to be put to death every person whom it shall have stricken with anathema.

ART. XXXIX.—The officers shall carry a dagger of antique form, the sub-officers and soldiers shall have guns, and bayonets, together with a poniard a foot long attached to their cincture, and upon which they will take oath, &c.

A large number of inspectors of police, generals, and statesmen, were assassinated by order of these tribunals. The lodges assisted in that work. Eckert says, *La Franc-Maçonnerie*, t. ii., p. 218, 219—"Mazzini was the head of that Young Europe and of the warlike power of Freemasonry, and we find in the Latomia that the minister Nothorub, who had retired from it, said to M. Vesbugem, even in the national palace in the presence of six deputies, that Freemasonry at the present time in Belgium had become a powerful and dangerous arm in the hands of certain men, that the Swiss insurrection had its resting place in the machinations of the Belgian lodges, and that Brother Defacqz, Grand Master of these lodges, had undertaken, in 1844, a voyage to Switzerland, only in order to prepare that agitation."

tyrants. But however much he laboured to make his terrible creed plausible, as being only permissible against tyrants and traitors, it was readily foreseen how easily it could be extended, until it became a capital danger for the sectaries themselves. Human nature could never become so base and so blinded as not to revolt against a principle so pernicious. It may last for a season amidst the first pioneers of the Alta Vendita, amongst the Black-Hand in Spain, amongst the Nihilists in Russia, amongst the Invincibles in Ireland, amongst the Trade-Unionists of the Bradlaugh stamp in England, or amongst the Communists of Paris. It may serve as a means to hold in terror the unfortunate prince or leader who may be seduced in youth or manhood to join secret societies from motives of ambition; and when that ambition was gratified, might refuse to go the lengths for Socialism which the Alta Vendita required. But otherwise assassination did not by experience prove such a sovereign power in the hands of the Carbonari as Mazzini expected. His more astute associates soon found out this; and not from any qualms of conscience, but from a strong sense of its inexpediency for their ends, they determined to reject it. They found out a more effective, though a far more infamous, way for attaining the dark mastery of the world. It was by the assassination not of bodies but of souls—by deliberate, systematic and persevering diffusion of immorality.[3]

The Alta Vendita, then, sat down calmly to consider the best means to accomplish this design. Satan and his fallen angels could devise no more efficacious methods than they found out. They resolved to spread impurity by every method used in the past by demons to tempt men to sin, to make the practice of sin habitual, and to keep the unhappy victim in the state of sin to the end. They had, being living men, means to accomplish this purpose, which devils could not use without the aid of men. Christian civilization established upon the ruins of the licentiousness of Paganism had kept European society pure. Vice, when it did appear, had to hide its head for shame. Public decency, supported by public opinion, kept it down. So long as morality existed as

[3] Nubius, who, in conjunction with the Templars of France, and the secret friends of the Revolution in England, had caused all the troubles endured by the Church and the Holy Father during the celebrated Congress of Rome and during the entire reign of Louis Philippe, and had so ably planned the revolutions afterwards carried out by Palmerston and Napoleon III, was written to before his death by one of his fellow-conspirators in the following strain:—"We have pushed most things to extremes. We have taken away from the people all the gods of heaven and earth that they had in homage. We have taken away their religious faith, their monarchical faith, their virtue, their probity, their family virtue; and, meantime, what do we hear in the distance but low bellowing; we tremble, for the monster may devour us. We have little by little deprived the people of all honourable sentiment. They will be without pity. The more I think on it the more I am convinced that we must seek delay of payment."

a recognized virtue, the Revolution had no chance of permanent success; and so the men of the Alta Vendita resolved to bring back the world to a state of brutal licentiousness not only as bad as that of Paganism, but to a state at which even the morality of the Pagans would shudder. To do this they proceeded with caution. Their first attempt was to cause vice to lose its conventional horror, and to make it free from civil punishment. The unfortunate class of human beings who make a sad trade in sin, were to be taken under the protection of the law, and to be kept free from disease at the expense of the State. Houses were to be licensed, inspected, protected, and given over to their purposes. The dishonour attached to their infamous condition was, so far as the law could effect it, to be taken away. That wholesome sense of danger and fear of disease which averted the criminally disposed from sin was to disappear. The agents of the Alta Vendita had instructions to increase the number and the seductiveness of those unfortunate beings, while the State, when revolutionized, was to close its eyes to their excesses, and to connive at their attempts upon the youth of the country. They were to be planted close to great schools and universities, and wherever else they could ruin the rising generation in every country in which the sect should obtain power.

Then literature was systematically rendered as immoral as possible, and diffused with a perseverance and labour worthy of a better cause. Railway stations, newspaper stands, book shops, and restaurants, were made to teem with infamous productions, while the same were scattered broadcast to the people over every land.

The teaching of the Universities and of all the middle schools of the State, was not only to be rendered Atheistic and hostile to religion, but was actually framed to demoralize the unfortunate alumni at a season of life always but too prone to vice.

Finally, besides the freest licence for blasphemy and immorality, and the exhibition and diffusion of immoral pictures, paintings, and statuary, a last attempt was to be made upon the virtue of young females under the guise of educating them up to the standard of human progress.

Therefore, middle and high-class schools were, regardless of expense, to be provided for female children, who should be, at any cost, taken far away from the protecting care of nuns. They were to be taught in schools directed by lay masters, and always exposed to such influences as would sap, if not destroy, their purity, and, as a sure consequence, their faith. These schools have since been the order of the day with Masonry all over the world. "If we cannot suppress woman let us corrupt her with the Church," said Vindex, and they have faithfully acted upon this advice.

The terrible society which planned these infernal means for destroying religion, social order, and the souls of men, continued its operations for many years. Its "permanent instruction" became the Gospel of all the secret societies of Europe. Its agents, like Piccolo Tigre, travelled unceasingly in every country. Its orders were received, according to the system of Masonry, by the heads and the rank and file of the lodges as so many inevitable decrees. But unfortunately for the world, it permitted too much political action to the second lines of the great conspiracy. In the latter, ambitious spirits arose, who, while embracing to the full the doctrines of Voltaire and the principles of Weishaupt, began to think that the Alta Vendita halted actual revolution too much. This state of feeling became general when that high lodge refused admittance to Mazzini, who wished to become one of the invisible forty—the number beyond which the supreme governing body never permitted itself to pass.

The jealousy of Nubius—for jealousy is a quality of demons not wanting from the highest intelligence in Atheistic organization to the lowest—prevented his being admitted. But he was already far too powerful with the rank and file of the Carbonari to be refused a voice in the supreme management. He raised a cry against the old chiefs as being impotent and needing change. Nubius consequently passed mysteriously away. M. Crétineau-Joly[4] is clearly of opinion that it was by poison; and as it was a custom with the unfortunate chief to betray for his own protection, or for punishment, some lodges of Carbonari to the Pontifical Government, it is more than probable that it was by his provision or information that the same Government came into the possession of the whole archives of the Alta Vendita, and that the Church and society have the documents which I have quoted and others still more valuable to guide them in discovering and defeating the attempts of organized Atheism.

The Alta Vendita subsequently passed to Paris, and since it is believed, to Berlin. It was the immediate successor of the Inner Circle of Weishaupt. It may change in the number of its adepts and in the places of its meetings, but it always subsists. There is over it, a recognized Chief like Nubius or Weishaupt. But in his lifetime this Chief is usually unknown, at least to the world outside "Illuminated" Masonry. He is unknown to the rank and file of the common lodges. But he wields a power which,

---

[4] Opus cit., ii, 23.

however, is not, as in the case of Nubius and Mazzini, always undisputed. Since that time, if not before it, there have been two parties under its Directory, each having its own duties, well defined.

XVI

THE INTELLECTUAL AND THE WAR PARTY IN MASONRY

ECKERT[1] shows that at present all secret societies
are divided into two parties—the party of direction
and the party of action or war party. The duty of
the intellectual party, is to plot and to contrive; that
of the party of action, is to combine, recruit, excite
to insurrection, and fight. The members of the war
party are always members of the intellectual party,
but not vice versa. The war party thus know what
is being plotted. But the other party, concealed as
common Freemasons amongst the simpletons of the
lodges, cover both sections from danger. If the war
party succeed, the peace party go forward and seize
upon the offices of state and the reins of power. Their
men go to the hustings, make speeches that suit, are

[1] La Franc-Maçonnerie dans sa véritable signification, par Eckert, avocat à Dresde,
trad. par Gyr (Liège 1854), t. I., p. 287; appendice. See also *Les Sociétés Révolutionnaires,
Introduction de faction des Sociétés Secrètes au xix. Siècle.* Par M. Claudio Jannel, Deschamps, Opus cit. xciii.

written up in the press, which, all the world over, is under Masonic influence. They are cried up by the adroit managers of mobs. They become the deputies, the ministers, the Talleyrands, the Fouchés, the Gambettas, the Ferrys; and of course they make the war party generals, admirals, and officers of the army, the navy, and the police. If the war party fails, the intellectual party, who close their lodges during the combat, appear afterwards as partisans, if possible, of the conquering party, or if they cannot be that, they silently conspire. They manage to get some friends into power. They agitate. They, in either case, come to the assistance of the defeated war party. They extenuate the faults, while condemning the heedless rashness of ill-advised, good-natured, though too ardent, young men. They cry for mercy. They move the popular compassion. In time, they free the culprits, and thus prepare for new commotions.

All Freemasonry has been long thus adapted, to enable the intellectual party to assist the war party in distress. It must be remembered that every Carbonaro is in reality a Freemason. He is taught the passes and can manipulate the members of the craft. Now, at the very threshold of the admission of a member to Freemasonry, the Master of the Lodge, the "Venerable," thus solemnly addresses him:—

"Masons," says he, "are obliged to assist each other by every means, when occasion offers. Freemasons ought not to mix themselves up in conspiracies; but if you come to know that a Freemason is engaged in any enterprise of the kind, and has fallen a victim to his imprudence, you ought to have compassion upon his misfortune, and the Masonic bond makes it a duty for you, to use all your influence and the influence of your friends, in order to diminish the rigour of punishment in his favour."

From this it will be seen, with what astute care Masonry prepares its dupes from the very beginning, to subserve the purposes of the universal Revolution. Under plea of compassion for a brother in distress, albeit through his supposed imprudence, the Mason's duty is to make use not only of all his own influence, but also "of the influence of his friends," to either deliver him altogether from the consequences of what is called "his misfortune," or "to diminish the rigour of his punishment."

Masonry, even in its most innocent form, is a criminal association. It is criminal in its oaths, which are at best rash; and it is criminal in promising obedience to unknown commands coming from hidden superiors. It always, therefore, sympathises with crime. It hates punishment of any repressive kind, and does what it can to destroy the death penalty even for murder. In revolution, its common practice is to open gaols, and let felons free upon society. When it cannot do this, it raises on their behalf a mock sympathy. Hence we have Victor Hugo pleading with every Government in Europe in favour of revolutionists; we have the French Republic liberating the Communists; and there is a motion before the French Parliament to repeal the laws against the party of dynamite—the Internationalists, whose aim is the destruction of every species of religion, law, order and property, and the establishment of absolute Socialism. With ourselves, there is not a revolutionary movement created, that we do not find at the same time an intellectual party apparently disconnected with it, often found condemning it but in reality supporting it indirectly but zealously. The Odgers and others of the Trades Union, for instance, will murder and burn; but it is the Bradlaughs and men theorising in Parliament if they can, or on the platform if they cannot, who sustain that very party of action. They secretly sustain what in public they strongly reprobate, and if necessary disown and denounce. This is a point worthy of deep consideration, and shows more than anything else, the ability and astuteness with which the whole organization has been planned.

Again, we must remember, that while the heads of the party of action are well aware of the course being taken by the intellectual party, it does not follow that the intellectual party know the movements of the party of action, or even the individuals, at least so far as the rank and file are concerned. It therefore can happen in this country, that Freemasons or others who are in communication only with the Supreme Council on the Continent, get instructions to pursue one line of conduct, and that the war party for deep reasons get instructions to oppose them. This serves, while preventing the possibility of exposure, to enable the work of the Infidel Propaganda to be better done. It is the deeply hidden Chief and his Council that concoct and direct all. They wield a power with which, as is well known, the diplomacy of every nation in the world must count. There are men either of this Council, or in the first line of its service, whom it will never permit to be molested. Weishaupt, Nubius, Mazzini, Piccolo Tigre, De Witt, Misley, Garibaldi, Number One, Hartmann, may have been arrested, banished, etc., but they never found the prison that could contain them long, nor the country that would dare deliver them up for crime against law or even life. It is determined by the Supreme Directory that at any cost, the men of their first lines shall not suffer; and from the beginning they have found means to enforce that determination against all the crowned heads of Europe. Now the man who succeeded to the Chieftaincy of this formidable conspiracy when Nubius passed away was none other than Lord Palmerston.

XVII

LORD PALMERSTON

IT is with difficulty that one can believe that Lord Palmerston knew the veritable secret of Freemasonry, and that for the greater part of his career he was the real master, the successor of Nubius, the Grand Patriarch of the Illuminati, and as such, the Ruler of all the secret societies in the world. As a Statesman, the distinguished nobleman had dealings of a very close character with Mazzini, Cavour, Napoleon III, Garibaldi, Kossuth, and the other leading revolutionary spirits of Europe in his day, but it was never for a moment suspected that he went so far as to accept the supreme direction of the whole dark and complex machinery of organized Atheism, or sacrificed the welfare of the great country he was supposed to serve so ably and so well, to the designs of the terrible secret conclave whose acts and tendencies were so well known to him. But the mass of evidence collected by Father Deschamps and others[1] to prove Lord Palmerston's complicity with the worst designs of Atheism against Christianity and monarchy—not even excepting the monarchy of England—is so weighty, clear, and conclusive, that it is impossible to refuse it credence. Father Deschamps brings forward in proof

[1] M. Eckert (opus cit.), was a Saxon lawyer of immense erudition, who devoted his life to unravel the mysteries of secret societies, and who published several documents of great value upon their action. He has been of opinion that "the interior order" not only now but always existed and governed the exterior mass of Masonry, and its cognate and subject secret societies. He says:—"Masonry being a universal association is governed by one only chief called a Patriarch. The title of Grand Master of the Order is not the exclusive privilege of a family or of a nation. Scotland, England, France, and Germany have in their time had the honour to give the order its supreme chief. It appears that Lord Palmerston is clothed to-day (Eckert wrote in Lord Palmerston's time) with the dignity of Patriarch.

"At the side of the Patriarch are found two committees, the one legislative and the other executive. These committees, composed of delegates of the Grand Orients (mother national lodges), alone know the Patriarch, and are alone in relation with him.

"All the revolutions of modern times prove that the order is divided into two distinct parties—the one pacific, the other warlike.

"The first employs only intellectual means—that is to say, speech and writing.

"It brings the authorities or the persons whose destruction it has resolved upon to succumb or to mutual destruction.

"It seeks for the profit of the order all the places in the State, in the Church (Protestant), and in the Universities; in one word, all the positions of influence.

"It seduces the masses and dominates over public opinion by means of the press and of associations.

"Its Directory bears the name of the Grand Orient and it closes its lodges (I will say why presently) the moment the warlike division causes the masses which they have won over to secret societies to descend into the street.

the testimony of Henry Misley, one of the foremost Revolutionists of the period, when Palmerston reigned over the secret Islam of the Sects, and other no less important testimonies. These I would wish, if time permitted, to give at length. But the whole history, unhappily, of Lord Palmerston proves them. In 1809, when but 23 years of age, we find him War Minister in the Cabinet of the Duke of Portland. He remained in this office until 1828, during the successive administrations of Mr. Percival, the Earl of Liverpool, Mr. Canning, Lord Goderick, and the Duke of Wellington. He left his party—the Conservatives—when

"At the moment when the pacific division has pushed its works sufficiently far that a violent attack has chances of success, then, at a time not far distant, when mens' passions are inflamed; when authority is sufficiently weakened; or when the important posts are occupied by traitors, the warlike division will receive orders to employ all its activity.

"The Directory of the belligerent division is called the Firmament.

"From the moment they come to armed attacks, and that the belligerent division has taken the reins, the lodges of the pacific division are closed. These tactics again denote all the ruses of the order.

"In effect, they thus prevent the order being accused of co-operating in the revolt.

"Moreover, the members of the belligerent division, as high dignitaries, form part of the pacific division, but not reciprocally, as the existence of that division is unknown to the great part of the members of the other division—the first can fall back on the second in case of want of success. The brethren of the pacific division are eager to protect by all the means in their power the brethren of the belligerent division, representing them as patriots too ardent, who have permitted themselves to he carried away by the current in defiance of the prescriptions of the order and prudence."

the last-named Premier insisted upon accepting the resignation of Mr. Huskisson. In 1830, he accepted the position of Foreign Secretary in the Whig Ministry of Earl Grey. Up to this period he must have been well informed in the policy of England. He saw Napoleon in the fulness of youth, and he saw his fall. He knew and approved of the measures taken after that event by the advisers of George IV, for the conservation of legitimate interests in Europe, and for the preservation for the Pope of the Papal States. The balance of power, as formed by the Congress of Vienna, was considered by the wisest and most patriotic English statesmen, the best safeguard for British interests and influence on the Continent. While it existed the multitude of small States in Italy and Germany could be always so manipulated by British diplomacy, as effectually to prevent that complete isolation which England feels to-day so keenly, and which may prove so disastrous within a short period to her best interests. If this sound policy has been since changed, it is entirely owing to Palmerston, who appears, after leaving the ranks of the Tories, to have thrown himself absolutely into the hands of that Liberalistic Freemasonry, which, at the period, began to show its power in France and in Europe generally. On his accession to the Foreign Office in 1830, he found the Cabinet freed from the influence of George IV, and from Conservative traditions: and he at once threw the whole weight of his energy, position and influence to cause his government to side with the Masonic programme for revolutionizing Europe. With his aid, the sectaries were able to disturb Spain, Portugal, Naples, the States of the Church, and the minor States of Italy. The cry for a constitutional Government received his support in every State of Europe, great and small. The Pope's temporal authority and every Catholic interest were assailed. England, indeed, remained quiet. Her people were fascinated by that fact. Trade interest being served by the distractions of other States, and religious bigotry gratified at seeing the Pope, and every Catholic country harassed, they all gave a willing, even a hearty support to the policy of Palmerston. They little knew that it was dictated, not by devotion to their interests, but in obedience to a hidden power of which Palmerston had become the dupe and the tool, and which permitted them to glory in their own quiet, only to gain their assistance and, on a future day, to compass with greater certainty their ruin. Freemasonry, as we have already seen, creates many "figure-head" Grand Masters, from the princes of reigning houses, and the foremost statesmen of nations, to whom, however, it only shows a small part of its real secrets. Palmerston was an exception to this rule. He was admitted into the very recesses of the Sect. He was made its Monarch, and as such ruled with a real sway over its realms of darkness. By this confidence he was flattered, cajoled, and finally entangled beyond the hope of extrication in the meshes of the sectaries. He was a noble, without a hope of issue, or of a near heir to his title and estates. He therefore preferred the designs of the Atheistic conspiracy he governed, to the interests of the country which employed him, and he sacrificed England to the projects of Masonry. As he advanced in years he appears to have grown more infatuated with his work. In 1837, in or about the time when Nubius was carried off by poison, Mazzini, who most probably caused that Chief to disappear, and who became the leader of the party of action, fixed his permanent abode in London. With him came also several counsellors of the "Grand Patriach", and from that day forward the liberty of Palmerston to move England in any direction, except in the interest of the secret conspiracy, passed away for ever. Immediately, plans were elaborated destined to move the programme of Weishaupt another step towards its ultimate completion.[2] These were, by the aid of well-planned Revolutions, to create one immense Empire from the small German States, in the centre of Europe, under the house of Brandenburg; next to weaken Austrian dominion; then to annihilate the temporal sovereignty of the Pope, by the formation of a United Kingdom of Italy under the provisional government of the house of Savoy; and lastly, to form of the discontented Polish, Hungarian, and Slavonian populations,

[2] In page 340, of his work, *Le Juif, &c*, already quoted, Gougenot des Mousseaux reproduces an article from the Political Blatter, of Munich, in 1862, in which is pointed out the existence in Germany, in Italy, and in London, of directing-lodges unknown to the mass of Masons, and in which Jews are in the majority. "At London, where is found the home of the revolution under the Grand Master, Palmerston, there exists two Jewish lodges which never permit Christians to pass their threshold. It is there that all the threads and all the elements of the revolution are reunited which are hatched in the Christian lodges." Further, des Mousseaux cites the opinion (p. 368) of a Protestant statesman in the service of a great German Power, who wrote to him in December, 1865, "at the outbreak of the revolution of 1845 I found myself in relation with a Jew who by vanity betrayed the secret of the secret societies to which he was associated, and who informed me eight or ten days in advance of all the revolutions which were to break out upon every point in Europe. I owe to him the immovable conviction that all these grand movements of 'oppressed people,' &c, &c, are managed by a half-a-dozen individuals who give their advice to the secret societies of the whole of Europe."

Henry Misley, a great authority also, wrote to Père Deschamps. "I know the world a little, and I know that in all that 'grand future' which is being prepared, there are not more than four or five persons who hold the cards. A great number think they hold them, but they deceive themselves."

an independent kingdom between Austria and Russia.

After an interval during which these plans were hatched, Palmerston returned to office in 1846, and then the influence of England was seen at work, in the many revolutions which broke out in Europe within eighteen months afterwards. If these partly failed, they eventuated at least in giving a Masonic Ruler to France in the person of the Carbonaro, Louis Napoleon. With him Palmerston instantly joined the fortunes of England, and with him he plotted for the realization of his Masonic ideas to the very end of his career. Now here comes a most important event, proving beyond question the determination of Palmerston to sacrifice his country to the designs of the Sect he ruled. The Conservative feeling in England shrank from acknowledging Louis Napoleon or approving of his coup d'etat. The country began to grow afraid of revolutionists, crowned or uncrowned. This feeling was shared by the Sovereign, by the Cabinet, and by the Parliament, so far that Lord Derby was able to move a vote of censure on the Government, because of the foreign policy of Lord Palmerston. For Palmerston, confiding in the secret strength he wielded, and which was not without its influence in England herself, threw every consideration of loyalty, duty, and honour overboard, and without consulting his Queen or his colleagues, he sent, as Foreign Secretary, the recognition of England to Louis Napoleon. He committed England to the Empire, and the other nations of Europe had to follow suit.

On this point Chambers' Encyclopædia, Art. "Palmerston," has the following notice:—"In December, 1852, the public was startled at the news that Palmerston was no longer a member of the Russell Cabinet. He had expressed his approbation of the coup d'etat of Louis Napoleon (gave England's official acknowledgment of the perpetration) without consulting either the Premier or the Queen; and as explanations were refused, Her Majesty exercised her constitutional right of dismissing her minister." Palmerston had also audaciously interpolated despatches signed by the Queen. He acted, in fact, as he pleased. He had the agents of his dark realm, in almost every Masonic lodge in England. The Press at home and abroad, under Masonic influences, applauded his policy. The Sect so acted that his measures were productive of immediate success. His manner, his bonhomie, his very vices fascinated the multitude. He won the confidence of the trading classes, and held the Conservatives at bay. Dismissed by the Sovereign, he soon returned into power her master, and from that day to the day of his death ruled England and the world in the interests of the Atheistic Revolution, of which he thought himself the master spirit.[3]

[3] Mr. F. Hugh O'Donnell, the able M.P. for Dungarvan, contributed to the pages of the Dublin Freeman's Journal a most useful and interesting paper which showed on his part a careful study of the works of Mgr. Ségur and other continental authorities on Freemasonry. In this, he says, regarding his own recollections of contemporary events:—"It is now many years since I heard from my lamented master and friend, the Rev. Sir Christopher Bellew, of the Society of Jesus, these impressive words. Speaking of the tireless machinations and ubiquitous influence of Lord Palmerston against the temporal independence of the Popes, Sir Christopher Bellew said:—'Lord Palmerston is much more than a hostile statesman. He would never have such influence on the Continent if he were only an English Cabinet Minister. But he is a Freemason and one of the highest and greatest of Freemasons. It is he who sends what is called the Patriarchal Voice through the lodges of Europe. And to obtain that rank he must have given the most extreme proofs of his insatiable hatred of the Catholic Church.'

"Another illustration of the manner in which European events are moved by hidden currents was given me by the late Major-General Burnaby, M.P., a quiet and amiable soldier, who, though to all appearance one of the most unobtrusive of men, was employed in some of the most delicate and important work of British policy in the East. General Burnaby was commissioned to obtain and preserve the names and addresses of all the Italian members of the foreign legion enlisted for the British service in the Crimean War. This was in 1855 and 1856. After the war these men, mostly reckless and unscrupulous characters—"fearful scoundrels" General Burnaby called them—dispersed to their native provinces, but the clue to find them again was in General Burnaby's hands, and when a couple of years later Cavour and Palmerston in conjunction with the Masonic lodges, considered the moment opportune to let loose the Italian Revolution, the list of the Italian foreign legion was communicated to the Sardinian Government and was placed in the hands of the Garibaldian Directory, who at once sought out most of the men. In this way several hundreds of "fearful scoundrels," who had learned military skill and discipline under the British flag, were supplied to Garibaldi to form the corps of his celebrated "Army of Emancipation" in the two Sicilies and

We shall see the truth of this when considering the political action of the Sect he led, but first it will be necessary to glance at what the Church and Christianity generally had to suffer in his day.

the Roman States. While the British diplomatists at Turin and Naples carried on, under cover of their character as envoys, the dangerous portion of the Carbonarist conspiracy, the taxpayers of Great Britain contributed in this manner to raise and train an army destined to confiscate the possessions of the Religious Orders and the Church in Italy, and, in its remoter operation, to assail, and, if possible, destroy the world-wide mission of the Holy Propaganda itself."

XVIII

WAR OF THE INTELLECTUAL PARTY

DURING what may be called the reign of Palmerston, the war of the intellectual party against Christianity, intensified in the dark counsels of the Alta Vendita, became accentuated and general throughout Europe. It chiefly lay in the propagandism of immorality, luxury, and naturalism amongst all classes of society, and then in the spread of Atheistic and revolutionary ideas. During the time of Palmerston's influence not one iota of the advices of the Alta Vendita was permitted to be wasted. Wherever, therefore, it was possible to advance the programme mapped out in the "Permanent Instruction," in the letter of Piccolo Tigre, and in the advices of Vindex, that was done with effect. We see, therefore, France, Italy, Germany, Spain, America, and the rest of the world, deluged with immoral novels, immodest prints, pictures, and statues, and every legislature invited to legalise a system of prostitution, under pretence of expediency, which gave security to sinners, and a kind of recognized status to degraded women. We find, wherever Masonry could effect it, these bad influences brought to bear upon the universities, the army, the navy, the training schools, the civil service, and upon the whole population. "Make corrupt hearts and you will have no more Catholics," said Vindex, and faithfully, and with effect, the secret societies of Europe have followed that advice. Hence, in France under the Empire, Paris, bad enough before, became a very pandemonium of vice; and Italy just in proportion to the conquests of the Revolution, became systematically corrupted on the very lines laid down by the Alta Vendita.

Next, laws subversive of Christian morality were caused to be passed in every State, on, of course, the most plausible pretexts. These laws were first that of divorce, then, the abolition of impediments to marriage, such as consanguinity, order, and relationship, union with a deceased wife's sister, etc. Well the Infidels knew that in proportion as nations fell away from the holy restraints of the Church, and as the sanctity and inviolability of the marriage bond became weakened, the more Atheism would enter into the human family.

Moreover, the few institutions of a public, Christian nature yet remaining in Christian States were to be removed one after another on some skilfully devised, plausible plea. The Sabbath which in the Old as well as in the New Dispensation, proved so great an advantage to religion and to man—to nations as well as to individuals—was marked out for desecration. The leniency of the Church which permitted certain necessary works on Sunday, was taken advantage of, and the day adroitly turned into one of common trading in all the great towns of Catholic Continental Europe. The Infidels, owing to a previous determination arrived at in the lodges, clamoured for permission to open museums and places of public amusement on the days sacred to the services of religion, in order to distract the population from hearing Mass and worshipping God. Not that they cared for the unfortunate working man. If the Sabbath ceased tomorrow, he would be the slave on Sunday that they leave him to be during the rest of the week. The one day of rest would be torn from the labouring population, and their lot drawn nearer than before to that absolute slavery which always did exist and would exist again, under every form of Idolatry and Infidelity. Pending the reduction of men to Socialism, the secret conclave directing the whole mass of organized Atheism has therefore taken care that in order to withdraw the working man from attending divine worship and hearing the Word of God, theatres, cafes, pleasure gardens, drinking saloons, and other still worse means of popular enjoyment shall be made to exert the utmost influence on him upon that day. This sad influence is beginning to be felt amongst ourselves. Then, besides the suppression of State recognition to religion, chaplains to the army, the navy, the hospitals, the prisons, etc., were to be withdrawn on the plea of expense or of being unnecessary. Courts of justice, and public assemblies were to be deprived of every Christian symbol. This was to be done on the plea of religion being too sacred to be permitted to enter into such places. In courts, in society, at dinners, etc., Christian habits, like that of grace before meals, etc., or any social recognition of God's presence, were to be scouted as not in good taste. The company of ecclesiastics was to be shunned, and a hundred other able means were devised to efface the Christian aspect of the nations until they presented an appearance more devoid of religion than that of the very pagans.

But of all the attacks made by Infidels during the reign of Palmerston, that upon primary, middle-class, and superior education was the most marked, the most determined, and decidedly, when successful, the most disastrous.

We must remember that from the commencement of the war of Atheism on Christianity, under Voltaire and the Encyclopædists, this means of doing mischief was the one most advocated by the chief leaders. They then accumulated immense sums to diffuse their own bad literature amongst every class. Under the Empire, the most disastrous blow struck by the Arch-Mason Talleyrand was the formation of a monopoly of education for Infidelity in the foundation of the Paris University. But it was left for the Atheistic plotters of this century to perfect the plan of wresting the education of every class and sex of the coming generations of men from out of the hands of the Church, and the influence of Christianity.

This plan was apparently elaborated as early as 1826, by intellectual Masonry. About that time appeared a dialogue between Quintex and Eugène Sue, in which after the manner of the letter of Vindex to Nubius the whole programme of the now progressing education war was sketched out. In this the hopes which Masonry had from Protestantism in countries where the population was mixed, were clearly expressed. The jealousy of rival Sects was to be excited, and when they could not agree, then the State was to be induced to do away with all kinds of religion "just for peace sake," and establish schools on a purely secular basis, entirely removed from "clerical control," and handed over to lay teachers, whom in time Atheism could find means to "control" most surely. But in purely Catholic countries, where such an argument as the differences of Sects could not be adduced, then the cry was to be against clerical versus lay teaching. Religious teachers were to be banished by the strong hand, as at present in France, and afterwards it could be said that lay teachers were not competent or willing to give religious instruction, and so that, too, in time, could be made to disappear.[1]

---

[1] The late celebrated Mgr. Dupanloup published, in 1875, an invaluable little treatise, in which he gave, from the expressions of the most eminent Masons in France and elsewhere, from the resolutions taken in principal lodges, and from the opinions of their chief literary organs, proofs that what is here stated is correct. The following extracts regarding education will show what Masonry has been doing in regard to that most vital question. Mgr. Dupanloup says:—"In the great lodge called the 'Rose of Perfect Silence,' it was proposed at one time for the consideration of the brethren:—'Ought religious education to be suppressed?' This was answered as follows:—'Without any doubt the principal of supernatural authority, that is faith in God, takes from a man his dignity, is useless for the discipline of children, and there is also in it, the danger of the abandonment of all morality' ... 'The respect, specially due to the child, prohibits the teaching to him of doctrines, which disturb his reason.'"

To show the reason of the activity of the Masons, all the world over, for the diffusion of irreligious education, it will be sufficient to quote the view of the Monde Maçonnique on the subject. It says, in its issue of May 1st, 1865, "An immense field is open to our activity. Ignorance and superstition weigh upon the world. Let us seek to create schools, professorial chairs, libraries." Impelled by the general movement thus infused into the body, the Masonic (French) Convention of 1870, came unanimously to the following decision:—"The Masonry of France associates itself with the forces at work in the country to render education gratuitous, obligatory, and laic."

One may here call to mind the fact that it was while Lord Palmerston directed Masonry as Monarch, and English policy as Minister, that an insidious attempt was made to introduce secularism into higher education in Ireland by Queen's Colleges, and into primary education by certain acts of the Board of National Education. The fidelity of the Irish Episcopacy and the ever vigilant watchfulness of the Holy See, disconcerted both plans, or neutralized them to a great extent. Attempts of a like kind are being made in England. There, by degrees, board

We have all heard how far Belgium has gone in pursuit of these Masonic aims at Infidel education. At one of the principal festivals of the Belgian Freemasons, a certain brother Boulard exclaimed, amidst universal applause. "When ministers shall come to announce to the country that they intend to regulate the education of the people I will cry aloud, 'to me a Mason, to me alone the question of education must be left, to me the teaching, to me the examination, to me the solution.'"

Mgr. Dupanloup also attacked the Masonic project of having professional schools for young girls, such as are now advocated in the Australian colonies and elsewhere in English-speaking countries. At the time, the movement was but just being initiated in France, but it could not deceive him. In a pamphlet, to which all the bishops of France adhered, and which was therefore called the Alarm of the Episcopate, he showed clearly that these schools had two faces, on one of which was written "Professional Instruction for Girls" and on the other, "Away with Christianity in life and death." "Without woman," said Brother Albert Leroy, at an International Congress of Masons, in Paris, in 1867, "all the men united can do nothing"—nothing to effectually de-Christianize the world.

But as we have seen the great aim of the Alta Vendita was to corrupt woman. "As we cannot suppress her," said Vindex to Nubius, "let us corrupt her with the Church." The method best adapted for this was to alienate her from religion by an infidel education.

schools with almost unlimited assistance from taxes have been first made legal, and then encouraged most adroitly. The Church schools have been systematically discouraged, and have now reached the point of danger. This has been effected, first, by the Masonry of Palmerston in high places, and secondly, by the Masonry of England generally, not in actual league and knowingly, with the dark direction I speak of, but unknowingly influenced by its well-devised cries for the spread of light, for the diffusion of education amongst the masses, for the banishment of religious discord, etc. It was, of course, never mentioned, that all the advantages cried up could be obtained, together with the still greater advantage of a Christian education, producing a future Christian population. It was sedulously kept out of sight that the people who would be certain to use board schools, were those who never went themselves to any church, and who would never think of giving religious instruction of any kind to their children. Nothing can show the power of Freemasonry in a stronger light than the stupor it was able to cast over the men who make laws in both Houses of the English Parliament, and who were thus hoodwinked into training up men fitted to take position, wealth, and bread itself, from themselves and their children; to subject, in another generation, the moneyed classes of England to the lot that befell other blinded "moneyed people" in France during the last century. In England, the Freemasons had, unfortunately, the Dissenters as allies. Hatred for church schools caused the latter to make common cause with Atheists against God, but the destruction of the Church of England—they do not hope for the destruction of the vigorous Catholic Church of the country— will never compensate even Socinians for a spirit of instructed irreligion in England—a spirit which, in a generation, will be able and only too willing to attempt Atheistic levelling for its own advantage, and certainly not for the benefit of wealthy Dissenters, or Dissenters having anything at all to lose.

The same influences of Atheism were potent, and for the same reasons, in all Australian legislatures. There the influence of continental Freemasonry is stronger than at home, and conservative influences which neutralize Atheistic movements of too democratic a nature in England and Scotland, are weaker. Hence, in all Australian Parliaments, Acts are passed with but a feeble resistance from the Church Party, abolishing religious education of every kind, and making all the education of the country "secular, compulsory and free." That is, without religion, enforced upon every class, and at the general expense of the State. Hence, after paying the taxation in full, the Catholic and the conscientious Christian of the Church of England, have to sustain in all those colonies their own system of education, and this, while paying for the other system, and while bearing the additional burden of the competition of State schools, richly and completely endowed with every possible requisite and luxury out of the general taxes.

A final feature in the education-war of Atheism against the Church especially, and against Christianity of every kind, is the attempted higher education without religion of young girls. The expense which they have induced every legislature to undertake for this purpose is amazing; and how the nations tolerate that expense is equally amazing. It is but carrying out to the letter the advice of Vindex:—"If we cannot suppress woman, let us corrupt her together with the Church." For this purpose those infamous hot-beds of foul vice, "lodges of adoption," lodges for women, and "androgynes,"—lodges for libertine Masons and women—were established by the Illuminati of France in the last century. For the same purpose schools for the higher education of young girls are now devised. This we know by the open avowal of leading Masons. They were introduced into France, Belgium, Italy, and Germany for the purpose of withdrawing young girls of the middle and upper classes from the blessed, safe control of nuns in convents, and of leading them to positive Atheism by Infidel masters and Infidel associates. This design of the lodges is succeeding in its mission of terrible mischief; but, thank God, not amongst the daughters of respectable Christians of any kind, who value the chastity, the honour, or the future happiness here and hereafter of that sex of their children, who need most care and delicacy in educating.

In the extract from the permanent instruction of the Alta Vendita, you have already seen how astutely the Atheists compassed the corruption of youth in Universities. It is since notorious that in all high schools over which they have been able to obtain influence, the students have been deprived of religion, taught to mock and hate it, allured to vicious courses, and have been placed under professors without religion or morality. How can we be surprised if the Universities of the Continent have become the hotbeds of vice, revolution, and Atheism? Moreover, when Masonry governs, as in France, Italy, and Germany, the only way for youth to obtain a livelihood on entering upon life is by being affiliated to Masonry; and the only way to secure advancement is to be devoted to the principles, the intrigues, and the interests of the Sect.

The continuous efforts of Masonry, aided by an immoral and Atheistic literature, by a corrupt public opinion, by a zealous Propagandism of contempt for the Church, for her ministers and her ministrations, and by a sleepless, able Directory devoted to the furtherance of every evil end, are enough in all reason to ruin Christianity if that were not Divine. But in addition to its intellectual efforts, Masonry has had from the beginning another powerful means of destroying the existing social and Christian order of the world in the interests of Atheism.

XIX

A WAR PARTY UNDER PALMERSTON

FATHER Deschamps, on the authority of Eckert and Misley, gives an interesting description of
all that Freemasonry, under the direction of Lord
Palmerston, attempted and effected after the failure of the revolutionary movements, conducted by
the party of action, under Mazzini, in 1848. These
were fomented to a large extent by British diplomacy and secret service money manipulated by Lord
Palmerston. Under his guidance and assistance,
Mazzini had organized all his revolutionary Sects.
Young Italy, Young Poland, Young Europe, and the
rest sprang as much from the one as from the other. But after years of close union, Mazzini, who was
probably hated by Palmerston, and dreaded as the
murderer of Nubius, began to wane in influence. He
and his party felt, of course, the inevitable effects
of failure; and the leader subsided without, however, losing any of his utility for the Sect. Napoleon
III appears to have supplanted him in the esteem of

Palmerston, and would, had he dared, have ceased to follow the Carbonari. Mazzini accordingly hated Napoleon III with a deadly hatred, which he lived to be able to gratify signally when Palmerston was no more. As he was the principal means of raising Palmerston to power in the Alta Vendita, so, after Palmerston had passed away, he introduced another great statesman, to the high conductors, if not into the high conduct itself, of the whole conspiracy; and caused a fatal blow to be given to France and to the dynasty of Napoleon. Meanwhile, from 1849 to the end of the life of Palmerston, the designs formed by the high council of secret Atheism, were carried out with a perfection, a vigour, and a success never previously known in their history. Nothing was precipitated; yet everything marched rapidly to realization. The plan of Palmerston—or the plan of the deadly council which plotted under him—was to separate the two great conservative empires of Russia and Austria, while, at the same time, dealing a deadly blow at both. It was easy for Palmerston to make England see the utility of weakening Russia, which threatened her Indian possessions. France could be made to join in the fray, by her ruler, and the powerful Masonic influence at his command: hence the Russian campaign of 1852. But it was necessary for this war to keep Prussia and Austria quiet, Prussia was bribed by a promise to get, in time, the Empire of United Germany. Austria was frightened by the resolution of England and France to bring war to the Danube, and so form a projected Kingdom in Poland and Hungary. The joint power of England, France, and Turkey could easily, then, with the aid of the populations interested, form the new kingdom, and so effectually curb Russia and Austria. But it was of more importance for the designs of the sect upon the temporal power of the Pope, and upon Austria herself, to separate the Empires. Palmerston succeeded with Austria, who withdrew from her alliance with Russia. The forces therefore of England and France, were ordered from the Danube to the barren Crimea, as payment for her neutrality. This bribe proved the ruin of Austrian influence. As soon as Russia was separated from her, and weakened beyond the power of assisting her, if she would, France, countenanced by England, dealt a deadly blow at Austrian rule in Italy, united Italy, and placed the temporal power of the Pope in the last stage of decay. On the other hand, Prussia was permitted to deal a blow soon after at Austria. This finished the prestige of the latter as the leading power in Germany, and confined her to her original territory, with the loss of Venice, her remaining Italian province. After this war, Palmerston passed away, and Mazzini came, once more, into authority in the Sect. He remembered his grudge against Napoleon, and at once used his influence with the high direction of Masonry to abandon France and assist Germany; and, on the promise of Bismarck—a promise fulfilled by the May laws—that Germany should persecute the Church as it was persecuted in Italy, Masonry went over to Germany, and Masons urged on Napoleon to that insane expedition which ended in placing Germany as the arbiter of Europe, and France and the dynasty of Napoleon in ruins. In the authorities quoted, there is abundant proof that Masonry, just as it had assisted the French Revolution and Napoleon I, now assisted the Germans. It placed treason on the side of the French, and sold in fact the unfortunate country and her unscrupulous ruler. Mazzini forced Italy not to assist Napoleon, and was gratified to find before his death, that the liar and traitor, who, in the hope of getting assistance he did not get from Masonry, had dealt his last blow at the Vicar of Christ, and placed Rome and the remnant of the States of the Church in the hands of the King of Italy, had lost the throne and gained the unenviable character of a coward and a fool.

This is necessarily but a brief glance at the programme, which Atheism has both planned and carried out since the rule of Palmerston commenced.

Wherever it prevailed, the worst form of persecution of the Church at once began to rage. In Sardinia, as soon as it obtained hold of the King and Government, the designs of the French Revolution were at once carried out against religion. The State itself employed the horrible and impure contrivances of the Alta Vendita for the corruption and demoralisation of every class of the people. The flood gates of hell were opened. Education was at once made completely secular. Religious teachers were banished. The goods of the religious orders were confiscated. Their convents, their land, their very churches were sold, and they themselves were forced to starve on a miserable pension, while a succession was rigorously prohibited. All recognition of the spiritual power of Bishops was put to an end. The priesthood was systematically despised and degraded. The whole ministry of the Church was harassed in a hundred vexatious ways. Taxes of a crushing character were levied on the administration of the sacraments, on masses, and on the slender incomes of the parish clergy. Matrimony was made secular, divorce legalised, the privileges of the clerical state abrogated. Worse than all, the *leva* or conscription was rigorously enforced. Candidates for the priesthood at the most trying season of their career, were compelled to join the army for a number of years, and exposed to all the

snares which the Alta Vendita had astutely prepared
to destroy their purity, and with it, of course, their
vocations; "make vicious hearts, and you will have
no more Catholics." Besides these measures made
and provided by public authority, every favour of
the State, its power of giving honours, patronage
and place, was constantly denied to Catholics. To
get any situation of value in the army, navy, civil
service, police, revenue, on the railways, in the tele-
graph offices, to be a physician to the smallest mu-
nicipality, to be employed almost anywhere, it was
necessary to be a Freemason, or to have powerful
Masonic influence. The press, the larger mercantile
firms, important manufactories, depending as such
institutions mostly do on State patronage and interest, were also in the hands of the Sectaries. To Catholics was left the lot of slaves. If permitted to exist
at all, it was as the hewers of wood and the draw-
ers of water. The lands which those amongst them
held, who did not forsake religion, were taxed to
an unbearable extent. The condition of the faithful
Catholic peasants became wretched from the load
of fiscal burdens placed upon them. The triumph
of Atheism could not be more complete, so far as
having all that the world could give on its side, and
leaving to the Church scarcely more than covered
her Divine Founder upon the Cross.

Bismarck, though assisted in his wars against France by the brave Catholic soldiers of the Rhine, and of the Fatherland generally, no sooner had his rival crushed, and his victory secured, than he hastened to pay to Freemasonry his promised persecution of the Church. The Freemasons in the German Parliament, and the Ministers of the Sect, aided him to prepare measures against the Catholic religion as drastic as those in operation in Italy, even worse in many respects. The religious orders of men and women were rigorously suppressed or banished, as a first instalment. Then fell Catholic education to make way for an Infidel propagandism. Next came harassing decrees against the clergy by which Bishops were banished or imprisoned and parishes were deprived in hundreds of their priests. All the bad, immoral influences, invented and propagated by the Sectaries, were permitted to run riot in the land. A schism was attempted in the Church. Ecclesiastical education was corrupted in the very bud, and all but the existence of Catholics was proscribed.

Wherever we find the dark sect triumphant we find the same results. In the Republics of South America, where Freemasonry holds the highest places, the condition of the Church is that of normal persecution and vexation of every kind. It has been so for many years in Spain and Portugal, in Swit-

zerland, and to whatever extent Freemasons can accomplish it, in Belgium and in Austria. The dark
Directory succeeding Weishaupt, the Alta Vendita,
and Palmerston, sits in Paris and in Berlin almost
openly, and prepares at leisure its measures, which
are nothing short of, first, the speedy weakening of
the Church, and then a bloody attempt at her exter-
mination. If it goes on slower than it did during the
French Revolution, it is in order to go on surer. Past
experience, too, and the determinations of the sect
already arrived at, show but too clearly that a single final consummation is kept steadily in view. The
impure assassins who conduct the conspiracy have
had no scruple to imbue their hands in the blood
of Christians in the past, and they never will have a
scruple to do so, whenever there is hope of success.
In fact, from what I have seen and studied on the
Continent, an attempt at this ultimate means of getting rid at least of the clergy and principal lay leaders amongst Catholics, might take place in France
and even in Italy at any moment. In France, some
new measure of persecution is introduced every day.
The Concordat is broken openly. The honour of the
country is despised. Subventions belonging by con-
tract to the clergy are withdrawn. The insolence of
the Atheistical Government, relying on the strength
of the army and on the unaccountable apathy or

cowardice of the French Catholic laity, progresses so fast, that no act of the Revolution of 1789 or of the Commune, can be thought improbable within the present decade; and Italy would be sure to follow any example set by France in this or in any other method of exterminating the Church.

There are sure signs in all the countries where the Atheistic Revolution has made decided progress, that this final catastrophe is planned already, and that its instruments are in course of preparation. These instruments are something the same as were devised by the illuminated lodges, when the power of the French Revolution began to pass from the National Assembly to the clubs. The clubs were the open and ultimate expression of the destructive, anti-Christianity of Atheism; and when the lodges reached so far, there was no further need for secrecy. That which in the jargon of the Sect is called "the object of the labour of ages," was attained. Man was without God or Faith, King or Law. He had reached the level aimed at by the Commune, which is itself the ultimate end of all Masonry, and all that secret Atheistic plotting which, since the rise of Atheism, has filled the world. In our day, if Masonry does not found Jacobite or other clubs, it originates and cherishes movements fully as Satanic and as dangerous. Communism, just like Carbonarism, is but a form of the illuminated Masonry of Weishaupt. "Our end," said the Alta Vendita, "is that of Voltaire and the French Revolution." Names and methods are varied, but that end is ever the same. The clubs at the period of the French Revolution were, after all, local. Masonry now endeavours to generalise their principles and their powers of destructive activity on a vastly more extended scale. We therefore no longer hear of Jacobins or Girondins, but we hear of movements destined to be for all countries what the Jacobins and the Girondins were for Paris and for France. As surely, and for the same purpose, as the clubs proceeded from the lodges in 1789, so, in the latter half of the nineteenth century, the lodges sent out upon the whole civilized world, for the very same intent, the terrible Socialist organizations, all founded upon the lines of Communism, and called according to the exigencies of time, place, and condition.

XX

THE INTERNATIONAL, THE NIHILISTS, THE BLACK HAND, &C.

THERE are multitudes in Freemasonry—even in the most "advanced" Freemasonry of Italy and France—who have no real wish to see the principles of these anarchists predominate. Those, for instance, who in advocating the theories of Voltaire, and embracing for their realization the organization of Weishaupt, saw only a means to get for themselves honours, power, and riches, which they could never otherwise obtain but by Freemasonry, would be well pleased enough to advance no further, once the good things they loved had been gained. "Nous voulons, Messieurs," said Thiers, "la république, mais la république conservatrice." He and his desired, of course, to have the Republic which gave them all this world had to bestow, at the expense of former possessors. They desired also the destruction of a religion which crossed their corrupt inclinations, and which was suspected of sympathy for the state of things which

Masonry had supplanted. But they had no intention, if they could help it, to descend again to the level of the masses from which they had sprung. In Italy, for instance, this class of Freemasons have had supreme power in their hands for over a quarter of a century. They obtained it by professing the strongest sympathy for the down-trodden millions whom they called slaves. They stated that these slaves—the bulk of the Italian people in the country and in the cities—were no better than tax-paying machines, the dupes and drudges of their political tyrants. Victor Emmanuel, when he wanted, as he said, "to liberate them from political tyrants," declared that a cry came to him from the "enslaved Italy," composed of these down-trodden, unregenerated millions. He and his Freemasons and Carbonari—the party of direction and the party of action—therefore drove the native princes of the people from their thrones, and seized supreme sway throughout the Italian peninsula. Were the millions of "slaves" served by the change? The whole property of the Church was seized upon. Were the burdens of taxation lightened? Very far from it. The change simply put hungry Freemasons, and chiefly those of Piedmont, in possession of the Church lands and revenues. It dispossessed many ancient Catholic proprietors, in order to put Freemasons in their stead. But with what consequence to the vast mass of the people, to the peasantry and the working population—some twenty-four out of the twenty-six millions of the Italian people? The consequence is this, that after a quarter of a century of vaunted "regenerated Masonic rule", during which "the liberators" were at perfect liberty to confer any blessings they pleased upon the people as such, the same people are at this moment more miserable than at any past period of their history, at least since Catholicism became predominant as the religion of the country. If their natural princes ever "whipped them with whips" for the good of the state, Freemasonry, under the House of Savoy, slashes them with scorpions, for the good of the fraternity. To keep power in the hands of the Atheists an army, ten times greater, and ten times more costly than before, had to be supported by the "liberated" people. A worthless but ruinously expensive navy has been created and must be kept by the same unfortunate "regenerated" people. These poor people, "regenerated and liberated," must man the fleets and supply the rank and file of Army and Navy; they must give their sons, at the most useful period of their lives, to the "service" of Masonic "United Italy." But the officials in both army and navy—and their number is legion—supported by the taxes of the people, are Freemasons or the sons of Freemasons. They vegetate in absolute uselessness, so far as the development of the country is concerned, living in comparative luxury upon its scanty resources. The civil service, like the army and navy, is swelled with "government billets," out of all proportion to the wants of the people. It is filled with Freemasons. It is a paradise of Freemasons, where Piedmontese patriots, who have intrigued with Cavour or fought under Garibaldi, enjoy *otium cum dignitate* at the expense of the hard earnings of a people very poor at any time, but by the present "regenerated" regime made more wretched and miserable than any Christian peasantry—not even excepting the peasantry of Ireland—on the face of the earth.

The consequence of the "liberation" wrought by the Freemasons in Italy is this: They clamoured for representative institutions. All their revolutions were made under the pretext that these were not granted—and the mass of Italian people—seven-eighths of them—are as yet unenfranchised, after a quarter of a century of Masonic supremacy in the land. The Masons represented the lot of the poor man as insupportable, under the native princes. But under themselves the poor man's condition, instead of being ameliorated, has been made unspeakably worse. He is positively, at present, ground down, in every little town of Italy, by insupportable exactions.

His former burdens are increased four-fold—in many cases, ten-fold. To find money for all the extravagances of Masonic rule—to make fortunes for the men at the top, and comfortable places for the rank and file of the sect, a system of taxation, the most elaborate, severe, and searching ever yet invented to crush a nation, has been devised. The peasant's rent is raised by Masonic greed whenever a Mason becomes a proprietor, as is often the case with regard to confiscated church lands. Land taxes cause the rents to rise everywhere. The tenant must bear them. Then every article of the produce of his little rented holding is taxed as he approaches the city gates to sell it. At home his pig is taxed, his dog, if he can keep one, his fowl, his house, his fireplace, his window light, his scanty earnings, *titulo servizio*, all are specially, and for the poor, heavily taxed. The consequence of this is, that few Italian peasants can, since Italy became "United," drink the wine they produce, or eat the wheat they grow. Flesh meat, once in common use, is now as rare with them, as it used to be with the peasantry in Ireland. Milk or butter they hardly ever taste. Their food, often sadly insufficient, is reduced to pizzi, a kind of cake made of Maize or Indian meal and vegetables or fruit when in season. Their drink is plain water. They are happy when they can mingle with it a little vinaccio, a liquid made after the grapes are pressed and the wine drawn off, by pouring water on the refuse. Their homes are cheerless and miserable, their children left to live in ignorance, without schooling, employed in coarse labour, and clothed in rags. The Grand Duke of Tuscany had by wise and generous regulations placed hundreds, yea, even thousands of these peasants, happy as independent farmers on their own land. The crushing load of taxation has caused these to disappear, and their little holdings have been sold by auction to pay taxes, and have passed, of course, into the hands of speculators, generally Freemasons, who, when they become landlords, vie with the worst of their class, in Ireland, in greed. In the States of the Church, where the careful, most Christian, and compassionate spirit and legislation of the Vicar of Christ prevailed, the peasantry ate their own bread, drank their own wine, and were decently, nay even picturesquely clad, as all travellers know, before the "liberation" of the Masonic Piedmontese. Not a family was without a little hoard of savings for the age of the old, and for the provision and placing in life of the young. Now, gaunt misery, even starvation, is the characteristic of these populations, after only some fifteen years of Masonic rule. The vast revenues of the Church are gone, none know wither. The nation is none the better for them, and the populace, in their dire poverty, can no longer go to the convent-gate, where before the poor never asked for bread in vain. The religious, deprived of their possessions, and severely repressed, have no longer food to give. They are fast disappearing, and the people already experience that the promises of Freemasonry, like the promises of its real author, are but apples of ashes, given but to lure, to deceive, and to destroy.

The Freemasonry of France and other Continental nations, which has done so much to give effect to the principles of Voltaire and Weishaupt, wishes decidedly not to go beyond the role played by the Freemasonry of Italy. But in France, as in Italy, an inexorable power is behind them, pushing them on, and also fanatically determined to push them off the scene when the time is ripe for doing so. This the Freemasons of Italy well know; this the men now in power in France feel. But if they move against the current coming upon them from the depths of Freemasonry, woe to them. The knife of the assassin is ready. The sentence of death is there, which they are too often told to remember, and which has before now reached the very foremost men of the sect who refused, or feared, for motives good or bad, to advance as quickly as the hidden chiefs of the Revolution desired and decreed. It "removed" Nubius in the days of Mazzini. It "removed" Gambetta before our eyes. It aimed frequently at Napoleon III and would most assuredly have struck home, but its aim was only to terrify him so that he as a Carbonaro would be made to do its work soon and effectively. Masonry obtained its end, and Napoleon marched to the Italian war, and to his doom.

It is this invisible power, this secret, sleepless, fanatical Directory, which causes the solidarity most evidently subsisting between Freemasonry in its many degrees and aspects and the various parties of anarchists which now arise everywhere in Europe. In the last century kings, princes, nobles, took up Masonry. It swept them all away before that century closed. In the beginning and progress of this century, the Bourgeoisie took it up with still greater zest, and made it all their own. For a long time they would not tolerate such a thing as a poor Mason. Poverty was their enemy. What has come to pass? The Bourgeoisie at this moment are the peculiar enemy of the class of workmen who have invaded "Black" or "Illuminated" Masonry, and made it at last completely theirs. The Bourgeoisie are now called upon by the Socialists to be true to the real levelling principles of the brotherhood—to practise as well as preach "liberty, equality, and fraternity;" to divide their possessions with the working men—to descend to that elysium of Masonry, the level of the Commune—or die.

It is strange how Masonry, being what it is, has always managed to get a princely or noble leader for every one of its distinct onward movements against princes, property, and society. It had Égalité to lead the movement against the throne of France in the last century. It had the Duke of Brunswick, Frederick II and Joseph II to assist. In this century we see it ornamented by Louis Philippe, Napoleon III, Victor Emmanuel and others as figure-heads; Nubius and Palmerston, both won from the leaders of the Conservative nobility, were its real chiefs. Now, when it appears in its worst possible form, it is championed by no less a personage than a Russian Prince, of high lineage, a representative of the wealthiest, most exclusive, and perhaps richest aristocracy in the world. We find that in all cases of seduction like this, the promise of mighty leadership has been the bait by which the valuable dupe has been caught by the sectaries. The advice of Piccolo Tigre for the seduction of princes has thus never been without its effect.

These new anarchial societies are not mere haphazard associations. They are most ably organised. There is, for instance, in the International, three degrees, or rather distinct societies, the one, however, led by the other. First come the International Brethren. These know no country but the Revolution; no other enemy but "reaction." They refuse all conciliation or compromise, and they regard every movement as "reactionary" the moment it ceases to have for its object, directly or indirectly, the triumph of the principles of the French Revolution. They cannot go to any tribunal other than a jury of themselves, and must assist each other, lawfully or otherwise, to the "very limits of the possible." No one is admitted who has not the firmness, fidelity, intelligence, and energy considered sufficient by the chiefs, to carry out as well as to accept the programme of the Revolution. They may leave the body, but if they do, they are put under the strictest surveillance, and any violation of the secret or indiscretion, damaging to the cause, is punished inexorably by death. They are not permitted to join any other society, secret or otherwise, or to take any public appointment without permission from their local committee; and then they must make known all secrets which could directly or indirectly serve the International cause.

The second class of Internationalists are the National Brethren. These are local socialists, and are not permitted even to suspect the existence of the International Brethren, who move among them and guide them in virtue of higher degree. They figure in the meetings of the society, and constitute the grand army of insurrection; they are, without knowing it, completely directed by the others. Both classes are formed strictly upon the lines laid down by Weishaupt.

The third class compromises all manner of workmen's societies. With these the two first mingle, and direct to the profit of the Revolution. The death penalty for indiscretion or treason is common in every degree.

The Black Hand and the Nihilists, are directed by the same secret agency, to violence and intrigue. Amongst them, but unknown to most of them, are the men of the higher degrees, who in dark concert, easily guide the others as they please. They administer oaths, plan assassinations, urge on to action, and terrorize a whole country, leaving the rank and file who execute these things to their fate. It is unnecessary to dwell longer upon these sectaries, well known by the outrages they perpetrate.

These terrible societies are unquestionably connected with, and governed by, the dark directory, which now, as at all times since the days of Weishaupt, rules the secret societies of the world. Mahommedanism permitted the assassins gathered under the "old man of the mountain," to assist in spreading the faith of Islam by terrorising its Chris-

tian enemies. For a like purpose, whenever it judges it opportune, the dark Alta Vendita employs the
assassins wholesale and retail of the secret societies.
It believes it can control when it pleases these ruth-
less enemies of the human race. In this, as Nubius
found out, it is far mistaken. But the encouragement of murderers as a "skirmishing" party of the
Cosmopolitan Revolution remains since the day of
Weishaupt—a policy kept steadily in view. To-day,
that party is used against some power such as that of
the Popes, or the petty princes of Italy. Great powers like England, in the belief that the mischief will
stop in Italy, rejoice in the results attained by assassination. To-morrow it suits the policy of the Alta
Vendita to make a blow at aristocracy in England, at
despotism in Russia, at monarchy in Spain; and at
once we find Invincibles formed from the advanced
amongst the Fenians; Nihilists and the Black Hand
from the ultras of the Carbonari; and Young Russia, ready to use dynamite and the knife and the revolver, reckless of every consequence, for the ends
of the secret directory with which the diplomacy of
the world has now to count. The professional lectures on the use and manufacture of dynamite given
to Nihilists in Paris, the numbers of them gathered
together in that capital, the retreat afforded them
there to the known murderers of the Emperor Alex-

ander, excited little comment in England. If referred to at all in the press, it was not with that vigorous abhorrence which such proceedings should create. Often a chuckle of satisfaction has been indulged in by some at the fact. The utterances of the "advanced" members of the Masonic Intellectual party in the French Senate excusing Nihilists, were quoted with a kind of "faint damnation" equivalent to praise. There is no doubt that in Russia a similar kind of tender treatment is given to the Fenian dynamitards employed by O'Donovan Rossa. So long as the leading nations in Europe do not see in these anarchists and desperate miscreants the irreconcilable enemies of the human race, Paris, completely Masonic as it is, will afford them a shelter; and when French tribunals fine or imprison them, it will be as in Italy with a tenderness still further exhibited in gaols. The salvation of Europe depends upon a manly abhorrence of secret societies of every description, and the pulling up root and branch from human society of the sect of the Freemasons whose "illuminated" plottings have caused the mischief so far, and which if not vigorously repressed by a decided union of Christian nations will yet occasion far more. *Deus fecit nationes sanabiles.* The nations can be saved. But if they are to be saved, it must be by a return to Christianity and to public Christian usages; by eradicating Atheism and its socialistic doctrines as crimes against the majesty of God and the well-being of individual men and nations; by rigorously prohibiting every form of secret society for any purpose whatever; by shutting the mouth of the blasphemer; by controlling the voice of the scoffer and the impure in the Press and in every other public expression; by insisting on the vigorous Christian education of children; and, if they can have the wisdom of doing it, by opening their ears to the warning voice of the Vicar of Jesus Christ. It is not an expression of Irish, discontent finding a vent in dynamite which England has most to fear from anarchy. Its value to the Revolution is the knowledge it gives to those millions whom English education-methods are depriving of faith in God, of the use of a terrible engine against order, property, and the very existence of the country as such. The dark directory of Socialism is powerful, wise and determined. It laughs at Ireland and her wrongs. It hates, and ever will hate, the Irish people for their fidelity to the Catholic faith. But it seizes upon those subjects which Irish discontent in America affords, to make them teach the millions everywhere the power of dynamite, and the knife, and the revolver, against the comparatively few who hold property. This is the real secret of dynamite outrages in England, in Russia, and all the world over;

and I fear we are but upon the threshold of a social convulsion which will try every nation where the wiles of the secret societies have obtained, through the hate of senseless Christian sectaries, the power for Atheism to dominate over the rising generation, and deprive it of Christian faith, and the fear and the love of God. I hope these my forebodings may not be realized, but I fear that even before another decade passes, Socialism will attempt a convulsion of the whole world equal to that of France in 1789; and that convulsion I fear this country shall not escape. Our only chance lies in a return to God, of which, alas, there are as yet but little signs amongst those who hold power amongst us. I mean of course a return to the public Christianity of the past.

To this pass Freemasonry has brought the world and itself. Its hidden Directory no outsider can know. Events may afterwards reveal who they were. Few can tell who is or is not within that dark conclave of lost but able men. There is no staying the onward progress of the tide which bears on the millions in their meshes to ruin. The only thing we can hope to do is to save ourselves from being deceived by their wiles. This, thank God, we may and will do. We can, at least, in compliance with the advice of our Holy Father, open the eyes of our own people, of our young men especially, to the nature and atrocity of the evil, that seeing, they may avoid the snare laid for them by Atheism. To do this with greater effect we shall now, for a while, consider the danger as it appears amongst ourselves.

FREEMASONRY WITH OURSELVES

WE hear from every side a great deal regarding the difference said to exist between Freemasonry as it has remained in the United Kingdom, and as it has developed itself on the Continent of Europe since its introduction there chiefly, we must remember, by British Jacobites, in the last century. It is argued, that the Illuminism of Weishaupt, or that of Saint Martin, did not cross the Channel to any great extent; and that on the whole the lodges of England, Ireland, and Scotland remained loyal to Monarchy and to religion. There is much truth in all this. The Conservative character of the mass of English Freemasons, and the fact, that amongst them were found the real governors and possessors of the country, made it impossible that such men could conspire against their own selves. But, as I have already shown, the fact that British lodges have always had intercourse with the lodges of the Continent,[1] makes it equally impossible that some, at least, of the theories of the latter should not have got into the lodges on this side of the water. I believe it is owing mainly to this influence over British Freemasons, that so many revolutionary movements have found favour with our legislators, who are, when they are not Catholics, generally of the craft. It was through it, that the fatal foreign policy of Lord Palmerston obtained such support, even against the conviction and instincts of the best and most farseeing statesmen of the country, as, for instance, the late Lord Derby. It was through it, certainly, that the cry for secular education was welcomed amongst us; that divorce and "liberal" marriage laws came into force, and that attacks

[1] A curious proof of this fact is preserved in the records of Dublin Castle, where, upon a return of the members and officers of Freemasonry, as it is with us, having been asked for by the Government, the names of the delegates from the Irish Lodges to various continental national Grand Lodges were given. I do not place much value upon the fact as a means to connect British Freemasonry with its kind on the Continent, because the REAL SECRET was, as a rule, kept from British and Irish Masons. But the intercourse had an immense effect in causing the vanguard cries of the Continental lodges to find a fatal support from British Masons in and out of Parliament. These delegates brought back high sounding theories about "education" without "denominationalism," etc., etc., but they were never trusted with the ultimate designs of the Continental directory to destroy the Throne, the Constitution, and lastly, the very property of British Masons. These designs are communicated only to reliable individuals, who know full well the REAL SECRET of the sect—and keep it.

were permitted upon the sanctity of the Sabbath and other Christian institutions.

The doing away by degrees of the "Lord's Day" is a favourite aim of Atheism; and it is by resisting this aim—by resisting all its aims on morality and religion that we can hope to sustain the Christianity and the religious character of this country and its people.[2]

[2] The Alta Vendita and the intellectual party in Masonry have for a long time endeavoured to revive practices which Christianity did away with, and which were distinctly pagan. Amongst others they have made every exertion to destroy the Christian respect for the dead, and every respect for the dead which kept alive in the living the belief in the immortality of the soul. Death is with man a powerful means to keep alive in him a wholesome fear of his Creator and respect for religion. Spiritual writers—following the advice of the Holy Ghost in the Scriptures, "Remember thy last end and thou shalt never sin," always place before Christians the thought of death as the most wholesome lesson in the spiritual life. The demon from the beginning tried to do away with this salutary thought as the most opposed to his designs. When Eve feared to eat the forbidden fruit it was because of the terror with which death inspired her. The devil lied in telling her, "No, ye shall not die the death." She believed the liar and the murderer. His followers in the secret societies established by him, and which he keeps in such unity of aim and action, second his desire to the utmost by doing away with whatever may keep alive in man the thoughts of his last end and of a future resurrection, and, of course, of judgment. Weishaupt taught his disciples to look upon suicide as a praiseworthy means of flying the horrors of death and present inconvenience. Cremation, instantly destroying the terrors of corruption—the death's head and cross-bones—the worst features in mortality, as exhibited in a corpse, is therefore largely advocated by the secret societies on plausibly devised sanitary, aesthetic, and economical grounds. But is it a pagan practice, opposed to that followed ever since the creation of the world by all that had the knowledge of the true God in the Primeval, Jewish, and Christian dispensations. The Revolution in Italy has established at Rome, Milan and Naples

But granting that British lodges remain unaffected by Atheism and Anti-Christianity which, as we have seen, influence the whole mass of Continental Freemasonry, would they on that account be innocent? Could a conscientious man of any Christian denomination join them? The question is, of course, decided for Catholics. The Church forbids her children to be members of British or any Freemasonry under penalty of excommunication. The reasons which have led the Church to make a law so stringent and so serious must have been very grave. We have seen some at least of these reasons; and it is certainly with a full knowledge of facts that she has decreed the same penalties against such of her children as join the English lodges as she has against those who join the lodges of the Continent. Then, though parsons have become "chaplains" to lodges, Anglicans generally have shown no sym-

means of cremating bodies, and advanced Freemasons, like Garibaldi, have in their wills, directed that their bodies should be cremated.

When in these days, a distinctive anti-Christian custom is seen advocated without any urgent reason in the press, now almost entirely in the hands of members of the Sect, and generally Jewish members, Christians may fear that the cloven foot is in the matter. The cold water, the ridicule, the contempt thrown upon religious observances, the attempt to rob them of their purely Christian character are other methods employed by the Sects to loosen the influence of Christianity. In opposition to these, Christian people should carefully study to keep the joy of Christmas, the penitential fasts, the sanctity of Holy Week, the splendour of Easter, the feasts of God's holy Mother and of the saints—to fill themselves, in one word, with the Christian spirit of the Ages of Faith.

pathy with the Freemasonry of England. I am not aware that Protestant denominations assume, or that their members grant them, the power of making laws which could bind in conscience. If they did possess such power, many of them, I have no doubt would forbid Freemasonry, as dangerous and evil in itself. But it needs not a law from man to guide one in determining what is clearly prohibited by reason and revelation. Now that which is called harmless Freemasonry with us, is, besides the evident danger to which it is exposed, of being made what it has become in the rest of the world, both sacrilegious and dangerous. If it be only a society for brotherly intercourse and mutual help, where can be the necessity of taking for such purposes, a number of oaths of the most frightful character? I shall now quote some of these oaths—the most ordinary ones taken by every English Freemason who advances to the first three degrees of the Craft. Oaths far more blasphemous and terrible are taken in the higher degrees both in England and on the Continent. I shall also give you the passwords, grips, and signs for these three main degrees. One can then judge of the nature of the travesty that is made of the name of God for purposes utterly puerile, if not meant to cover such real and deadly secrecy as that of Continental Masonry. The first of these oaths is administered to the candidate who wishes to become an apprentice. He is divested of all money and metal. His right arm, left breast and left knee are bare. His right heel is slipshod. He is blindfolded, and a rope called a "cable tow," adapted for hanging, is placed round his neck. A sword is pointed to his breast, and in this manner he is placed kneeling before the Master of the Lodge, in whose presence he takes the following oath, his hand placed on a Bible:—

"I, N. N., in the presence of the great Architect of the Universe, and of this warranted, worthy and worshipful lodge of free and accepted Masons, regularly assembled and properly dedicated, of my own free will and accord, do hereby and hereon, most solemnly and sincerely swear, that I will always hail, conceal, and never reveal, any part or parts, point or points, of the secrets and mysteries of, or belonging to, free and accepted Masons in masonry, which have been, shall now, or hereafter may be, communicated to me, unless it be to a true and lawful brother or brothers, and not even to him or them, till after due trial, strict examination, or sure information from a well-known brother, that he or they are worthy of that confidence, or in the body of a just, perfect, and regular lodge of accepted Freemasons. I further solemnly promise, that I will not write those secrets, print, carve, engrave, or otherwise delineate them, or cause or suffer them to be done so by others, if in my power to prevent it, on anything movable or immovable under the canopy of heaven, whereby or whereon any letter, character or figure, or the least trace of a letter, character or figure may become legible or intelligible to myself, or to anyone in the world, so that our secrets, arts, and hidden mysteries, may improperly become known through my unworthiness. These several points I solemnly swear to observe, without evasion, equivocation, or mental reservation of any kind, under no less a penalty, on the violation of any of them, than to have my throat cut-across, my tongue tom out by the root, and my body buried in the sand of ike sea at low water mark, or a cable's length from the shore, where the tide regularly ebbs and flows twice in the twenty-four hours, or the more efficient punishment of being branded as a wilfully perjured individual, void of all moral worth, and unfit to be received in this warranted lodge, or in any other warranted lodge, or society of Masons, who prize honour and virtue above all the external advantages of rank and fortune: so help me, God, and keep me steadfast in this my great and solemn obligation of an Entered Apprentice Freemason."

W. M.—"What you have repeated may be considered a sacred promise as a pledge of your fidelity, and to render it a solemn obligation, I will thank you to seal it with your lips on the volume of the sacred law." (Kisses the Bible.)

When the above oath is duly taken, the "sign" is given. This for an Apprentice, consists of a gesture made by drawing the hand smartly across the throat and dropping it to the side. This gesture has reference to the penalty attached to breaking the oath. The grip is also a penal sign. It consists of a distinct pressure of the top of the right hand thumb to the first joint from the wrist of the right hand forefinger, grasping the finger with the hand. The pass-word is BOAZ, and is given letter by letter.

There are a number of quaint ceremonial charges and lectures which may be seen by consulting any of the Manuals of Freemasonry, and which are perfectly given in a treatise by one Garble, an Atheist, who undertook for the benefit of Infidelity to divulge the whole of the mere ceremonial secrecy of English Freemasons, in order to advance the real secret of it all, namely Pantheism or Atheism, and hatred for every form of Christianity. The English Freemasons made too much of the ceremonies and too little of Atheism, and hence the design of real Infidelity to get the "real secret" into English lodges by expelling the pretended one.

The oath of the second degree, that of Fellow-Craft, is as follows:—

"I, N. N., in the presence of the Grand Geometrician of the Universe, and in this worshipful and warranted Lodge of Fellow-Craft Masons, duly constituted, regularly assembled, and properly dedicated, of my own free will and accord, do hereby and hereon most solemnly promise and swear that I will always hail, conceal, and never reveal any or either of the secrets or mysteries of, or belonging to, the second degree of Freemasonry, known by the name of the Fellow-Craft, to him who is but an entered Apprentice, no more than I would either of them to the uninitiated or the popular world who are not Masons. I further solemnly pledge myself to act as a true and faithful craftsman, obey signs, and maintain the principles inculcated in the first degree. All these points I most solemnly swear to obey, without evasion, equivocation, or mental reservation of any kind, under no less a penalty, on the violation of any of them, in addition to my former obligation, than to have my left breast cut open, my heart tom therefrom, and given to the ravenous birds of the air, or the devouring beasts of the field, as a prey: so help me Almighty God, and keep me steadfast in this my great and solemn obligation of a Fellow-Craft Mason."

After taking this oath with all formality, the Fellow-Craft Mason is entrusted with the sign, grip and pass-word by the Master, who thus addresses him:—

"You, having taken the solemn obligation of a Fellow-Craft Freemason, I shall proceed to entrust you with the secrets of the degree. You will advance towards me as at your initiation. Now take another pace with your left foot, bringing the right heel into its hollow, as before. That is the second regular step in Freemasonry, and it is in this position that the secrets of the degree are communicated. They consist as in the former instance, of a sign, token, and word; with this difference that the sign is of a three-fold nature. The first part of a three-fold sign is called the sign of fidelity, emblematically to shield the repository of your secrets from the attacks of the cowan. (The sign is made by pressing the right hand on the left breast, extending the thumb perpendicularly to form a square). The second part is called the hailing sign, and is given by throwing the left hand up in this manner (horizontal from the shoulder to the elbow, and perpendicular from the elbow to the ends of the fingers, with the thumb and forefinger forming a square.) The third part is called the penal sign, and is given by drawing the hand across the breasts and dropping it to the side. This is in allusion to the penalty of your obligation, implying that as a man of honour, and a Fellow-Craft Mason, you would rather have your heart tom from your breast, than to improperly divulge the secrets of this degree. The grip, or token, is given by a distinct pressure of the thumb on the second joint of the hand or that of the middle finger. This demands a word; a word to be given and received with the same strict caution as the one in the former degree, either by letters or syllables. The word is JACHIN. As in the course of the evening you will be called on for this word, the Senior Deacon will now dictate the answers you will have to give."

The next oath is that of the highest substantial degree in old Freemasonry, namely, that of Master. Attention is specially to be paid to the words "or at my own option."

"I, N. N., in the presence of the Most High, and of this worthy and worshipful lodge, duly constituted, regularly assembled, and properly dedicated, of my own free will and accord, do hereby and hereon, most solemnly promise and swear, that I will always hail, conceal, and never reveal, any or either of the secrets or mysteries of, or belonging to, the degree of a Master Mason, to anyone in the world, unless it be to him or them to whom the same may justly and lawfully belong; and not even to him or them, until after due trials, strict examination, or full conviction, that he or they are worthy of that confidence, or in the bosom of a Master Mason's Lodge. I further most solemnly engage that I will keep the secrets of the Third Degree from him who is but a Fellow-Craft Mason, with the same strict caution as I will those of the Second Degree from him who is but an Entered Apprentice Freemason; the same or either of them, from anyone in the known world, unless to true and lawful Brother Masons. I further solemnly engage myself to advance to the pedestal of the square and compasses, to answer and obey all lawful signs and summonses sent to me from a Master Mason's Lodge, if within the length of my cable-tow, and to plead no excuse except sickness, or the pressing emergency of my own private or public avocations. I furthermore solemnly pledge myself to maintain and support the five points of fellowship, in act as well as in word; that my hand given to a Mason shall be the sure pledge of brotherhood; that my foot shall traverse through danger and difficulties, to unite with his in forming a column of mutual defence and safety; that the posture of my daily supplications shall remind me of his wants, and dispose my heart to succour his distresses and relieve his necessities, as far as may fairly be done without detriment to myself or connexions; that my breast shall be the sacred repository of his secrets, when delivered to me as such; murder, treason, felony, and all other offences contrary to the law of God, or the ordinances of the realm, being at all times most especially excepted or at my own option: and finally, that I will support a Master Mason's character in his absence as well as I would if he were present. I will not revile him myself, nor knowingly suffer others to do so; but will boldly repel the slander of his good name, and strictly respect the chastity of those that are most dear to him, in the persons of his wife, sister, or his child: and that I will not knowingly have unlawful carnal connexion with either of them. I furthermore solemnly vow and declare, that I will not defraud a Brother Master Mason, or see him defrauded of the most trifling amount, without giving him due and timely notice thereof; that I will also prefer a Brother Master Mason in all my dealings, and recommend him to others as much as lies in my power, so long as he shall continue to act honourably, honestly and faithfully towards me and others. All these several points I promise to observe, without equivocation or mental reservation of any kind, under no less a penalty, on the violation of any of them, than to have my body severed in two, my bowels torn thereout, and burned to ashes in the centre, and those ashes scattered before the four cardinal points of heaven, so that no trace or remembrance of me shall be left among men, particularly among Master Masons: So help me God, and keep me steadfast in this grand and solemn obligation, being that of a Master Mason."

A long ceremony follows, in which the newly-made Master is made to sham a dead man and to be raised to life by the Master, grasping, or rather clawing his hand or wrist, by putting his right foot to his foot, his knee to his knee, bringing up the right breast to his breast, and with his hand over the back. This is practised in Masonry as the five points of Fellowship.

Then the Master gives the signs, grip, and password, saying:

"Of the signs, the first and second are casual, the third is penal. The first casual sign is called the sign of horror, and is given from the Fellow-Craft's hailing sign, by dropping the left hand and elevating the right, as if to screen the eyes from a painful sight, at the same time throwing the head over the right shoulder, as a remove or turning away from that sight. It alludes to the finding of our murdered Master Hiram by the twelve Fellow-Crafts. The second casual sign is called the sign of sympathy or sorrow, and is given by bending the head a little forward, and by striking the right hand gently on the fore-head. The third is called the penal sign, because it alludes to the penalty of your obligation, and is given by drawing the hand across the centre of the body, dropping it to the side, and then raising it again to place the point of the thumb on the navel. It implies that, as a man of honour and a Master Mason, you would rather be severed in two than improperly divulge the secrets of this Degree. The grip or token is the first of the five points of fellowship. The five points of fellowship are: first, a grip with the right hand of each other's wrist, with the points of the fingers; second right foot parallel with right foot on the inside; third, right knee to right knee; fourth, right breast to right breast; fifth, hand over shoulder, supporting the back. It is in this position, and this only, except in open lodge, and then but in a whisper, that the word is given. It is MAHABONE or MACBENACH. The former is the ancient, the latter the modern word."

I have here given an idea of the principal ceremonies used in making English Freemasons. I could not in the space I have allotted to myself, enter, as I would wish to do, upon other features of its ridiculous rites and observances, many of which in still higher degrees, get a gradually opening, Atheistic and most anti-Christian interpretation. But it will suffice for my purpose to bring one fact under your observation. In the ceremonies accompanying initiations, many charges are made to the candidates and lectures and catechisings are given. In these, in the highest degrees, the real secret is gradually divulged in a manner apparently the most simple. For instance in the degree of the Knights Adepts of the Eagle or the Sun, the Master in his charge describing the Bible, Compass, and Square, says:—

"By the Bible, you are to understand that it is the only law you ought to follow. It is that which Adam received at his creation, and which the Almighty engraved in his heart. This law is called natural law, and shows positively that there is but one God, and to adore only him without any sub-division or interpolation. The Compass gives you the faculty of judging for yourself, that whatever God has created is well, and he is the sovereign author of everything. Existing in himself, nothing is either good or evil, because we understand by this expression an action done which is excellent in itself, is relative, and submits to the human understanding, judging to know the value and price of such action, and that God, with whom everything is possible, communicates nothing of his will but such as his great goodness pleases; and everything in the universe is governed as he has decreed it with justice, being able to compare it with the attributes of the Divinity. I equally say, that in himself there is no evil, because he has made everything with exactness, and that everything exists according to his will; consequently, as it ought to be. The distance between good and evil, with the Divinity, cannot be more justly and clearly compared than by a circle formed with a compass: from the points being reunited there is formed an entire circumference; and when any point in particular equally approaches or equally separates from its point, it is only a faint resemblance of the distance between good and evil, which we compare by the points of a compass, forming a circle, which circle, when completed, is God!"

From this it will be clear, to what the so-called veneration for the Bible and for religion comes to, at last, in all Freemasonry. From apparent agreement with Christianity it ends in Atheism. In the essentially Jewish symbolism of Masonry, the Trinity is ignored from the commencement, and God reduced to a Grand Architect. The mention of Christ is carefully avoided. By degrees the Bible is not revelation at all—only the laws written on the heart of every man by the one God—the one God, yet, however, somewhat respected. But in a little while, we find the "one God" reduced to very small dimensions indeed. You may judge for yourself by the Compass that God exists in himself, "therefore"—though it is hard here to see the therefore—"nothing is either good or evil." Here is a blow at the moral law. Finally, "God," spoken of with such respect in all the preceding degrees, is reduced to a nonentity—"which circle when completed is God." This is a perfect introduction on Weishaupt's lines to Weishaupt's Pantheism.

But the theories of Masonry, however developed, do less practical mischief than the conduct it fosters. The English, happily for themselves, are, in many useful respects, an eminently inconsistent people. The gentry amongst them can join Freemasonry and yet keep, in the most illogical manner possible, their very diluted form of Christianity. It has been otherwise with the more reasoning Continental Masons. They either abandon the Craft or abandon their Christianity. But the morality inculcated by Freemasonry has done immense damage in English-speaking countries nevertheless. The very oath binding a Master Mason to respect the chastity of certain near relations of another Master Mason, insinuates a wide field for licence; and Masons, even in England, have never been the most moral of men. It leads them, we too well know, to the neglect of home duties, and it leads them to an unjust persecution of outsiders, for the benefit of Craftsmen—a matter more than once complained of as injurious in trade, politics, and social life. I need not call to your mind what mischief—what foul murder—it has led to in America. I prefer to let Carlile, the Infidel apologist of dark Masonry, speak on this point. He says:—

"My exposure of Freemasonry in 1825 led to its exposure in the United States of America; and a Mason there of the name of William Morgan, having announced his intention to assist in the work of exposure, was kidnapped under pretended forms and warrants of law, by his brother Masons, removed from the State of New York to the borders of Canada, near the falls of Niagara, and there most barbarously murdered. This happened in 1826. The States have been for many years much excited upon the subject; a regular warfare has arisen between Masons and anti-Masons;—societies of anti-Masons have been formed; newspapers and magazines started; and many pamphlets and volumes, with much correspondence, published; so that, before the Slavery Question was pressed among them, all parties had merged into Masons and anti-Masons. Several persons were punished for the abduction of Morgan; but the murderers were sheltered by Masonic Lodges, and rescued from justice. This was quite enough to show that Masonry, as consisting of a secret association, or an association with secret oaths and ceremonies, is a political and social evil."

While writing this, I have been informed that individual members of Orange Lodges have smiled at the dissolution of their lodges, with the observation, that precisely the same association can be carried on under the name of Masonry. This is an evil that secret associations admit. No form of anything of the kind, when secret, can protect itself from abuses; and this is a strong reason why Masonic associations should get rid of their unnecessary oaths, revise their constitutions, and throw themselves open to public inspection and report. There is enough that may be made respectable in Masonry, in the present state of mind and customs, to admit of scrutinising publicity.

The question of the death of Morgan, and other unhappy incidents in the history of Freemasonry in the United States, are very fully treated by Father Muller, C.SS.R. Yet, strange to say, notwithstanding anti-Masonic societies being formed extensively in the Great Republic, and the horror created by the murder of Morgan, there is no part of the world where Masonry flourishes more than in America. I believe it will yet become the greatest enemy of the free institutions of that country. I am willing to admit, however, that Freemasonry has, thank God, made little progress amongst Catholics in Ireland, or Catholics of Irish birth or blood anywhere. This is true, and the same may be said of millions of Protestants who have not joined Masonry. But the evil is amongst us for all that, and it is necessary that we should know what it is and how it manifests itself.

We know too, that besides the movements which Masonry has been called upon to serve by means of Masonic organs, and resolutions inspired by Atheism, and advocated by its hidden friends scattered through British lodges, there have been at all times, at least in London, some lodges affiliated to Continental lodges, and doing the work of Weishaupt. Of this class were several lodges of foreigners and Jews, which existed in London contemporaneously with Lord Palmerston, and which aided him in the government and direction of the secret societies of the world, and in the Infidel Revolution which was carried on during his reign with such ability and success. In the works of Deschamps, a detailed account will be found of several of these high temples of iniquity and deadly, anti-Christian intrigue. But besides Masonry of any description—and every description, for reasons already stated, even the most apparently harmless, is positively bad—bad, because of its oaths, because of its associations, and because of its un-Christian character, there were other societies formed on the lines of Illuminated Masonry under various names in Great Britain, and especially in Ireland, of which I deem it my duty while treating of the subject to speak as plainly as I possibly can.

XXII

FENIANISM

FROM the establishment of Illuminated Masonry, its Supreme Council never lost sight of a discontented population in any part of the earth. Aspiring to universal rule, it carefully took cognizance of every national or social movement among the masses, which gave promise of advancing its aims. It was thus it succeeded with the operative and peasant population of France, so as to accomplish the first and every subsequent revolution in that country. The letters of the Alta Vendita and of Piccolo Tigre especially, have carefully had in view the corruption of the masses of working men, so as to de-Christianize them adroitly, and fit and fashion them into revolutionists. Now amongst all the peoples of the earth, those who most impeded Atheistic designs, were the Catholics of Ireland. Forced to leave their country in millions, they brought to Scotland, to England, to the United States, to Canada, to the West Indies, to our growing Colonies—all empires in germ—of

Australia, and as soldiers of England, to India, Africa and China, the strongest existing faith in that very religion which Atheistic Freemasonry so much desires to destroy. It would be impossible to imagine, that the dark Directories of the Illuminati did not take careful account of this population. And they did. In the years preceding 1798, they had emissaries, like those sent subsequently amongst the Catholic Carbonari of Naples, active amongst the ranks of the United Irishmen. France, then completely under the control of the Illuminati, sent aid which she sorely wanted at home, at the instigation of these very emissaries, to found an Irish Republic, of course on the Atheistic lines, upon which all the Republics then founded by her arms were established. That expedition ended in failure; but organisations on the lines of Freemasonry continued for many years afterwards to distract Ireland. As in Italy, the Illuminati had taught the peasantry of Ireland how to conspire in secret, oath bound, and, of course, often murderous, but always hopeless, league against their oppressors. These societies never accomplished one atom of good for Ireland. They did much mischief. But what cared the hidden enemies of religion for the real happiness of the Irish? Their gain consisted in placing antagonism between the faithful pastors of the people and the members of those secret societies of Ribbonmen, Molly Maguires, and other such associations, organized by designing and, generally, traitorous scoundrels. In 1848, there was something like a tendency in Ireland to imitate the secret revolutionary movements established on the Continent by Mazzini. We had a Young Ireland Organization. That was not initiated as a secret society. Neither was the Society of United Irishmen at first. But the open United Irishmen led to the secret society; and so very easily might the Young Ireland movement of 1848, if it had not been prematurely brought to a conclusion. As it was, it led, without its leaders desiring it—indeed against the will of many of them—to the deepest, most cunningly devised, widespread, and mischievous, secret organization into which heedless young Irishmen have been ever yet entrapped. This was the Fenian Secret Society.

We can speak of the action of the originators of this movement as connected with the worst form of Atheistic, Continental, secret-society organization; for they boasted of having gone over to France "to study" the plans elaborated by the most abandoned revolutionists in that country. For my own part, I believe that these hot-headed young men, as they were at the time, never took the initiative themselves, but were entrapped into this course of action by agents of the designing Directory of the Atheistic movement, at that moment presided over by Lord Palmerston himself. That the association of the Fenians should be created and afterwards sacrificed to England, would be but in keeping with the tradition of the Alta Vendita, in whose place Lord Palmerston and his council stood. We read in the life of the celebrated Nubius, the monarch who preceded Palmerston, that he often betrayed into the hands of the Pontifical Government some lodges of the Carbonari under his own rule, for the purpose of screening himself and of punishing those very lodges. If he found a lodge indiscreet, or possessing amongst its members too much religion to be tractable enough to follow the Infidel movement, he betrayed it. He told the Government how to find it out; where it had its arms concealed; who were its members; and what were their misdeeds. They were accordingly taken red-handed, tried, and executed. Nubius got rid of a difficult body, for whom he felt nothing but contempt; and his position at Rome was rendered secure to gnaw, as he himself expressed it, at the foundations of that Pontifical power, which thought that any connection such a respectable nobleman as he was, might have with assassins, could be only in reality for the good of religion and the government, to which by station, education, and even class-interest he was allied. Palmerston, too, if he wanted a blind to lead his colleagues astray, could, in the knowledge to be obtained of Fenian plots in Ireland and America, have a ready excuse for his well-known, constant intercourse with the heads of the Revolution of the world. What scruple would he have, any more than his predecessor, Nubius, in urging on a few men whom he despised, to revolution; and then using means to strangle their efforts and themselves if necessary? It was good policy in the sight of some at least of his colleagues, to manifest Ireland as revolutionary, especially when such a man as Palmerston had all the threads of the conspiracy which aimed at the revolution in his hand. They knew that he knew where to send his spies, and thwart at the opportune moment the whole movement. He could cause insurrections to be made in the most insane manner, as to time and place, just as they were made, and cover the conspirators with easy defeat and ridicule.

However this may be, the Fenian movement after being nursed in America, appeared in Ireland, as a society founded upon lines not very unlike those of the Carbonari of Italy. It was Illuminated Freemasonry with, of course, another name, in order not to avert the pious Catholic men it meant to seduce and destroy from its ranks. But being what it was, it could not long conceal its innate, determined hostility to the Catholic religion; and it proved itself in

Ireland, and wherever it took a hold of the people in the three kingdoms, one of the most formidable enemies to the souls of the Irish people that had ever appeared.

When I say this, do not imagine that I mean for a single moment to infer, that many of those who joined it, held or knew its views. If all I have hitherto stated proves anything, it is this: the nature of the infernal conspiracy which we are considering is essentially hypocritical. It comes as Freemasonry comes, with a lie in its mouth. It comes under false pretences always. So it came to Italy under the name of Carbonarism. It came, not only professing the purest Catholic religion, but absolutely made the saying of prayers, the frequentation of the sacraments, the open confession of the Faith, and devotion to the Vicar of Christ, a matter of obligation. I do not believe that Fenianism came to Ireland with so many pious professions. But it came in the guise of patriotism, which in Ireland, for many centuries, was so bound up with religion that in the minds of the peasantry the one became inseparably connected with the other. The friend of the one was looked upon as the friend of the other; and the enemy of the one was regarded as the enemy of the other. Hence, in the minds of the Irish, in my own boyhood, the French who came over under Hoche, were regarded as Catholic. The Irish held, that France was then as she was when the "wild geese" went over to fight for the Bourbons, a Catholic nation. The truth was, of course, quite the opposite; but so long had the Irish people been accustomed to regard the French as Catholic, that they still cherished the delusion, and would hear or believe nothing to the contrary. It was enough, therefore, for Fenianism to appear in the guise of a national movement meant to free the country from Protestant England, that it should without question be looked upon as—at least in the first instance— essentially Catholic. Nevertheless, after its leaders had gone to Paris to study the methods of the French and Italian Carbonari, and returned to create circles and centres on the plan of the Vendita of the Italians, they showed a large amount of the Infidel spirit of the men they found in France, and determined to spread it in Ireland. They well knew that the Catholic clergy would be sure to oppose and denounce them as would every wise and really patriotic man in the country. The utter impossibility of any military movement which could be made by any available number of destitute Irish peasantry succeeding at the time, was in itself reason enough why man of any humanity, not to speak at all of the clergy, should endeavour to dissuade the people from the mad enterprise of the Fenians. Every good and experienced Irishman, Smith O'Brien, the editors of the *Nation* and others, did so; yet strange to say, the leaders of the disastrous movement, the Irish, and the American organizers, were permitted by the English Government, at least so long as Lord Palmerston lived, to act almost as they pleased in Ireland. The Government knew, that while impotent to injure England, these agitators and conspirators were doing the work which English anti-Catholic hate desired to do, more effectively than any delusion, or bribe, or persecution which heresy had been able to invent. They were undermining the Faith of the people and destroying secretly but surely that love and respect for the clergy which had distinguished the country ever since the days of St. Patrick. A paper edited by one of these men was circulated for at least two years in the homes of nearly all the population. It contained, to be sure, much incitement to revolution; but it contained also that which in Lord Palmerston's eyes compensated for the kind of revolution Fenians could make a thousand fold—it contained the most able, virulent, and subtle attacks upon the clergy. This paper remained undisturbed until Palmerston passed away and affairs in America made Fenianism a real danger for his successors in office. Its issues contained letters written in its own office, but purporting to come from various country parishes, calumniating many of the most venerable of the priests of the people. Men who so loved their flocks as to sacrifice all for them during the famine years—men who had lived with them from youth to old age, were now so artfully assailed as foes of their country's liberation, that the people, maddened and deluded by such attacks, passed them on the road without the usual loving salutation Catholics in Ireland give to and receive from their priests. The Sect backed up the action of the newspaper. Its leaders got the "word of command" for that purpose, and had to be obeyed. Matters proceeded daily from bad to worse, until at last Divine Providence manifested clearly the deadly designs against religion underlying the Fenian movement, and the people of Ireland recoiled from it and were saved.

It was hard to keep even the leaders themselves bad to the end. At death, few of them like to face the God they have outraged without reconciliation. But in life these men, like the informers with whom they are so often in alliance, do desperate things to deceive first, and then, for a passing interest, to ruin their unfortunate dupes afterwards. For my own part, I am of opinion that the man who deludes a number of brave young hearts to rush into a murderous enterprise, hopeless from the outset, is as dangerous as the man who seduces men to become assassins and then sacrifices their lives to save his own neck from the halter. At most there is but the difference of degree in the guilt and malignity of the leaders who urged on impetuous youth to such risings as those of the snowstorms in 1867, and of the scoundrel who planned assassination, entrapped and excited the same kind of youth to execute it, and then swore their lives away to save him s elf from his justly deserved doom. I am led to this conclusion inevitably from the account given of the Fenian rising by one of the purest Irish patriots of this century, one just gone amidst the tears of his fellow-countrymen, with stainless name after a career of glorious labour, to his eternal reward. Mr. Alexander M. Sullivan in his interesting *Story of Ireland*, says:

"There was up to the last a fatuous amount of delusion maintained by the 'Head Centre' on this side of the Atlantic, James Stephens, a man of marvellous subtlety and wondrous powers of plausible imposition; crafty, cunning, and quite unscrupulous as to the employment of means to an end. However, the army ready to hand in America, if not utilized at once, would soon be melted away and gone, like the snows of past winters. So in the middle of 1865 it was resolved to take the field in the approaching autumn.

"It is hard to contemplate this decision or declaration without deeming it either insincere or wicked on the part of the leader or leaders, who at the moment knew the real condition of affairs in Ireland. That the enrolled members, howsoever few, would respond when called upon, was certain at any time; for the Irish are not cowards; the men who joined this desperate enterprise were sure to prove themselves courageous, if not either prudent or wise. But the pretence of the revolutionary chief, that there was a force able to afford the merest chance of success, was too utterly false not to be plainly criminal.

"Towards the close of 1865 came almost contemporaneously the Government swoop on the Irish Revolutionary executive, and the deposition—after solemn judicial trial, as prescribed by the laws of the society—of O'Mahony, the American 'Head Centre' for crimes and offences alleged to be worse than mere imbecility, and the election in his stead of Colonel William R. Roberts, an Irish American merchant of high standing and honourable character, whose fortune had always generously aided Irish patriotic, charitable, or religious purposes. The deposed official, however, did not submit to the application of the society rules. He set up a rival association, a course in which he was supported by the Irish Head Centre; and a painful scene of factious and acrimonious contention between the two parties thus antagonised, caused the English Government to hope—nay, for a moment—fully to believe—that the disappearance of both must soon follow."

Mr. A. M. Sullivan, after speaking of the history of the Fenian movement in America, continues:—

"This brief episode at Ridgeway was for the confederated Irish the one gleam to lighten the page of their history for 1866. That page was otherwise darkened and blotted by a record of humiliating and disgraceful exposures in connection with the Irish Head Centre. In autumn of that year he proceeded to America, and finding his authority repudiated and his integrity doubted, he resorted to a course which it would be difficult to characterize too strongly. By way of attracting a following to his own standard, and obtaining a flush of money, he publicly announced that in the winter months close at hand, and before the new year dawned, he would (sealing his undertaking with an awful invocation of the Most High) be in Ireland, leading the long-promised insurrection. Had this been a mere 'intention' which might be 'disappointed,' it was still manifestly criminal thus to announce it to the British Government, unless, indeed, his resources in hand were so enormous as to render England's preparations a matter of indifference. But it was not as an 'intention' he announced it and swore to it. He threatened with the most serious personal consequences any and every man soever, who might dare to express a doubt that the event would come off as he swore. The few months remaining of the year flew by; his intimate adherents spread the rumour that he had sailed for the scene of action, and in Ireland the news occasioned almost a panic. One day, towards the close of December, however, all New York rang with the exposure that Stephens had never quitted for Ireland, but was hiding from his own enraged followers in Brooklyn. The scenes that ensued were such as may well be omitted from these pages. In that bitter hour thousands of honest, impulsive and self-sacrificing Irishmen endured the anguish of discovering that they had been deceived as never had men been before; that an idol worshipped with frenzied devotion was, after all, a thing of clay."

The plottings of the "Head Centre," however, were not at an end. Mr. A. M. Sullivan continues:—

"In Ireland, where Stephens had been most implicitly believed in, the news of this collapse—which reached her early in 1867—filled the circles with keen humiliation. The more dispassionate wisely rejoiced that he had not attempted to keep a promise, the making of which was in itself a crime; but the desire to wipe out the reproach supposed to be cast on the whole enrolment by his public defection became so over-powering, that a rising was arranged to come off simultaneously all over Ireland on the 5th March, 1867.

"Of all the insensate attempts at revolution recorded in history, this one assuredly was pre-eminent. The most extravagant of the ancient Fenian tales supplies nothing more absurd. The inmates of a lunatic asylum could scarcely have produced a more impossible scheme. The one redeeming feature in the whole proceeding was the conduct of the hapless men who engaged in it. Firstly, their courage in responding to such a summons at all, unarmed and unaided as they were. Secondly, their intense religious feeling. On the days immediately preceding the 5th March, the Catholic churches were crowded by the youth of the country, making spiritual preparations for what they believed would be a struggle in which many would fall and few survive. Thirdly, their noble humanity to the prisoners whom they captured, their scrupulous regard for private property, and their earnest anxiety to carry on their struggle without infraction in aught of the laws and rules of honourable warfare."

XXIII

CONCLUSION

IN conclusion, it is proper that I should say a word to you upon the attitude of the Church at the present moment, in the face of the forces of the Organized Atheism of the world. That organization has now arrived at the perfection of its dark wisdom, and is making rapid strides to the most complete and universal exercise of its power. It has succeeded. Through it the Church is despoiled … The religious orders are virtually suppressed in nearly every country of Europe. Freemasonry is supreme in the governments of France, Spain, Portugal, Italy, and Switzerland, and works its will in nearly all the Republics of Southern America. It rules Germany, terrifies Russia, distracts Belgium, and secretly gnaws at the heart of Austria.[1] Everywhere it advances with

---

[1] According to the Rev. Humphrey J. T. Johnson in "Freemasonry, A Short Historical Sketch" (*Catholic Truth Society*, July, 1950):—

In Italy, "Mussolini showed himself an implacable opponent of the order" while "in Germany, the Fuhrer, convinced that not only Humanitarian but Christian masonry as well was permeated by the Judaic spirit, suppressed the latter, as well as the former,

rapid strides both in its secret movements against Catholicism and the Christian religion generally, and in open persecution according to the measure of its opportunity and power. No hope, humanly speaking, appears on the horizon to warrant us at this moment to look for a change for the better. But God has promised never to desert His Church. That promise never can be broken. When the darkest hour comes it is not for Catholics to look for dissolution, but for life and hope. The crisis in the conflicts of Christianity is the hour of victory.

By his immortal Bull, *Humanum Genus*, Leo XIII has dealt a death blow to the progress of Freemasonry, which exerted the utmost efforts of every kind to keep itself hidden. That it had power to remain hidden is looked upon by some as one of the most remarkable evidences of its real power … Exposure is its death—the death at least of its influence over its intended dupes amongst Catholics. Therefore comes the word of command to us all … :—"Tear off the

and would not even allow its Grand Lodges to continue a nominal existence under such names as the National Christian Order of Frederick the Great or the Order of Friendship."

Father Johnson also points out that "with the defeat of the Axis powers the anti-masonic movement collapsed."

In Spain under General Franco and in Portugal under Dr. Salazar, Freemasonry is forbidden in spite of efforts by American Nato representatives to establish lodges there.

mask from Freemasonry and make plain to all what it really is." Consequently it becomes a plain duty, in season and out of season, to expose Freemasonry.

Printed in Great Britain
by Amazon

45186757R00139